THE JOHN BUTLER TRIO SONGBOOK
VOL 2 – SELECTIONS FROM GRAND NATIONAL

Exclusive Distributor for Australia & New Zealand:
Music Sales Pty. Limited
Unit 1, 20 Resolution Drive
Caringbah NSW 2229, Australia

This book © Copyright 2007
By Wise Publications
ISBN 1-92102 90 3X
ISBN 13: 978 1921 0290 35
Order No. MS04136

Printed by Southwood Press Pty Ltd
Design by Ben Lurie
Arrangements by Tom Farncombe
Music arranged by Arthur Dick
Music processed by Paul Ewers Music Design
Edited by Tom Farncombe
Photos – James Minchin

www.johnbutlertrio.com

Unauthorised reproduction of any part
of this publication by any means including
photocopying is an infringement of copyright.

Wise Publications
Part of The Music Sales Group
London/NewYork/Sydney/Paris/Copenhagen/Madrid

CONTENTS

6	BETTER THAN	36	GOOD EXCUSE
13	DANIELLA	41	DEVIL RUNNING
20	FUNKY TONIGHT	48	LOSING YOU
29	CAROLINE	56	FIRE IN THE SKY

Everyone looking
but you cannot see

Got your eyes open
but you cannot see
Oh Caroline.

Got what you want
do you got what you need
Oh Caroline.

Looking for something
that you cannot find
Oh Caroline

Look at in front
and you look from behind
Oh Caroline.

All one day you see something
that you cannot bear
Oh Caroline

Take it from me girl
you better beware
Oh Caroline.

Her papa loved her
like nothing you can
Oh Caroline

Loved her a little too much
if you know what I mean
Oh Caroline.

So she left home young
and roamed from town to town
Oh Caroline

FUNKY TONIGHT (WHATS YOUR NAME)

WHATS YOUR NAME?
LETS GO BACK TO WHEN WE
FIRST MET BACK 1999
'PRECIATE!
BEFORE YOU KNEW I WAS
YOURS (YOU MINES)
AND I KNEW YOU WERE MINE

(CHORUS #1

WHATS YOUR NAME
DONT REFRAIN
YOU & NOW WE'RE ONE
IN TH SAME.
THE WAY YO SHAKKING
THAT DRIVES ME STRAIGHT UP INSANE

BETTER THAN

WORDS & MUSIC BY JOHN BUTLER

Tuning
6 = D 3 = G
5 = G 2 = B
4 = D 1 = D

Verse (Em⁷)

1. 3. All you want is what you can't have and if you
2. All the time while you're looking a-way there are

(G)

just look a-round, man, you see you got ma - gic. So just
things you can do, man, there's things you can say - a to the

(Em⁷)

sit back re - lax, en - joy it while you still have it. Don't
the ones you're with, with whom you're spend - ing the day. And get your

(G)   *To Coda* ⊕

look back on life, man and on - ly see tra - gic, here you go.
gaze off to - mor - row and come what may. Oh be - cause.
(3.) be - cause.

Gtrs. 1+2 (acous.)

Tacet 3°

Chorus

(Em⁷) You can be better than that, (don't) let it get the better of you.

(G) What could be a better than now? Life's not about what's better than.

(Em⁷) You can be better than that, (don't) let it get the better of you.

(G) What could be a better than now? Life's not about what's better. | -bout what's better.

Bridge

(G/C)
(Asus2)
All I know some -
(Gadd9)
(G/F♯)
- times things can be hard. But
(G/C)
(Asus2)
you should know by
(Gadd9)
(G/F♯)
now they come and they go. So
T
A
B

why, oh why do I look to the other side? 'Cos I know the grass is greener but just as hard to mow.

11

DANIELLA

WORDS & MUSIC BY JOHN BUTLER

Tuning
6 = C 3 = G
5 = G 2 = C
4 = C 1 = E

© COPYRIGHT 2007 FAMILY MUSIC PROPRIETARY LIMITED.
ALL RIGHTS RESERVED. INTERNATIONAL COPYRIGHT SECURED.

Verse
(C)
(E♭)
(1. 3.) up__ lit - tle girl like the 4th of Ju - ly, I love you more than ev' - ry sin - gle star,man,
(2.) day__ that I asked your par - ents for your hand and near - ly knocked them off their feet, they could a
w/percussive groove + Fig. 1
Tacet 2°+3°
(F)
(C)
in the sky. You are the best__ damn thing that ev - er hap - pened to me, I wan - na
hard - ly stand. The same day__ I asked you be my wife to__ be, I said my
(E♭)
(F)
(C)
take you home and then start mak - ing fam - i - l - y. You are a damn fine la - dy like a
m, m, m, m, m, m, m, m, mar - ry__ me. I said I prom - ise to love you and__
Play all times, sim. ad lib. 2°+3°
(2°)
8vb
slow slide
(E)
(F)
no oth - er, want to in - tro - duce you to my fa - ther and my mo - ther. I'm so
treat you right,__ give you the pro - per res - pect you de - serve ev - 'ry day and night.__ Give__ you

(C)
(E♭)
damn hap-py you want to be my lov - er, can't wait to get you home and get you
good and good lov-in' 'til the mor-nin' light and I pro-mise we will ne-ver ev-er
TAB
Pre chorus
(F)
(F)
(E♭)
un-der the cov - ers. Be-cause (1, 2.) Dan - i - ell - a, be my Cin - de - rel - la, won't you
ev - er fight. Yeah, right, yeah. (3.) Dan - i - ell - a, sweet as the sun, oh won't you
TAB
(B♭)
(F)
come on in a-round and a be - a my - o ba - by. Dan - i - ell - a, don't
come on in a-round and a be - a my - o ba - by. Dan - i - ell - a, be
TAB
(E♭)
To Coda
(B♭)
1.
N.C.
you re-mem-ber?
my Cin - der-rel - a.
Won't you come? Yeah!
TAB

Chorus
(C)
(E♭)
Dan - i - el - la, oh, doh, doh, doh, doh, doh, doh, doh, Dan - i - el - la, oh
(F)
(C)
doh, doh, doh, doh, doh, Dan - i, Dan - i - el - la, oh, doh, doh, doh, doh, doh, doh, doh,
(E♭)
(B♭)
2.
Dan - i - el - la. I re - mem - ber Yeah!
slide off
Solo
(C)
(E♭)
(F)
gradual bend
ff w/wah and dist.
full

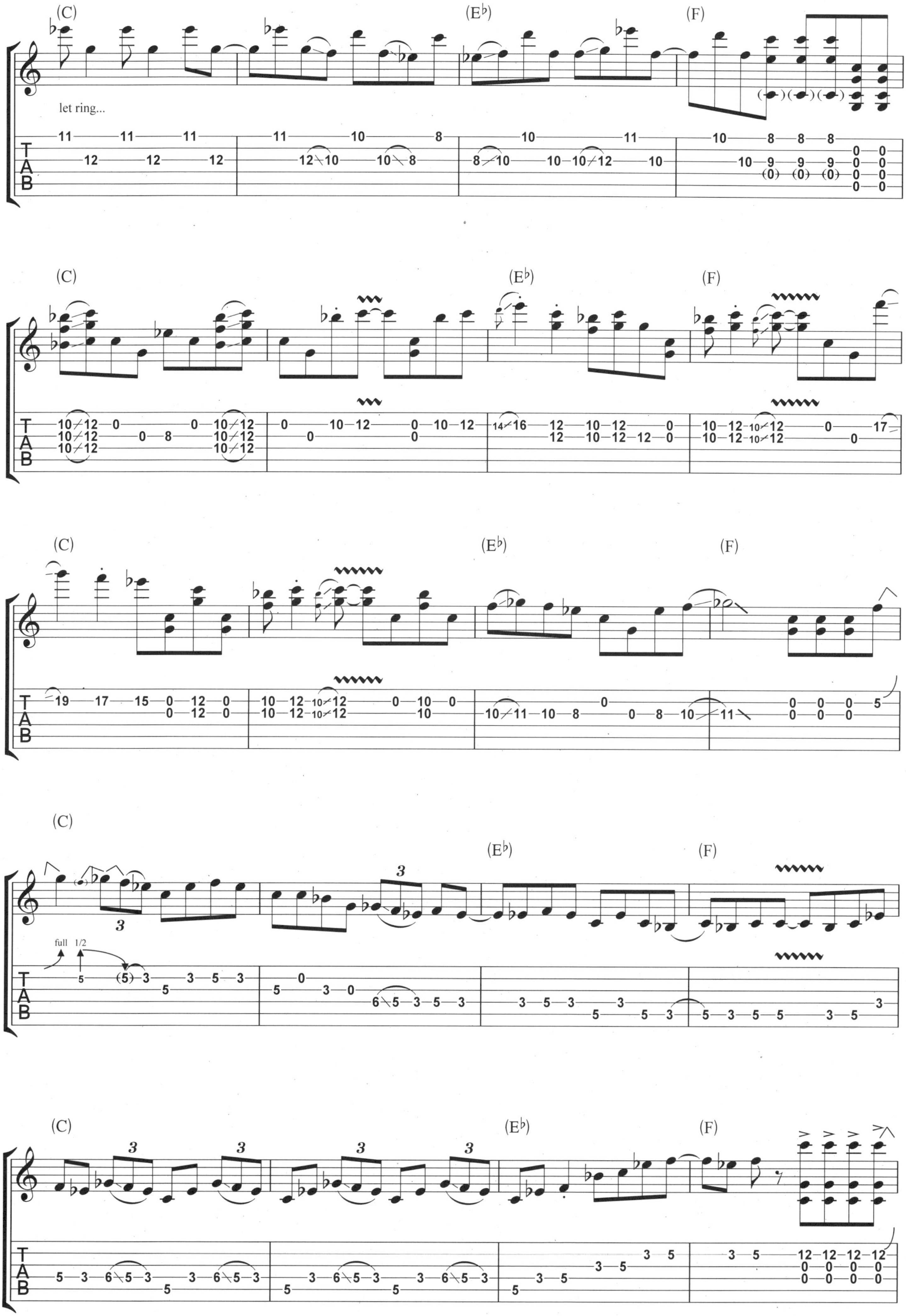
(C)
(E♭)
(F)
let ring...
(C)
(E♭)
(F)
(C)
(E♭)
(F)
(C)
(E♭)
(F)
full
1/2
(C)
(E♭)
(F)

3. You light me

Coda
(B♭)
N.C.
Won't you come? Yeah!
Outro Chorus
1, 2, 3.
(C)
(E♭)
Dan - i - el - la, oh, doh, doh, doh, doh, doh, doh, doh. Dan - i - el - la, oh
4.
(F)
(E♭)
(F)
doh, doh, doh, doh, doh, Dan - i. Dan - i - el - la, call me.
N.C.
(1°)
Play 3 times
Dan - i - el - la.
Percussion groove
TAB

FUNKY TONIGHT

WORDS & MUSIC BY JOHN BUTLER

Tuning
6 = C   3 = G
5 = G   2 = C
4 = C   1 = E
Capo 4th fret

Intro ♩ = 142

Gtr. 1 (amplified 11-string acous.)

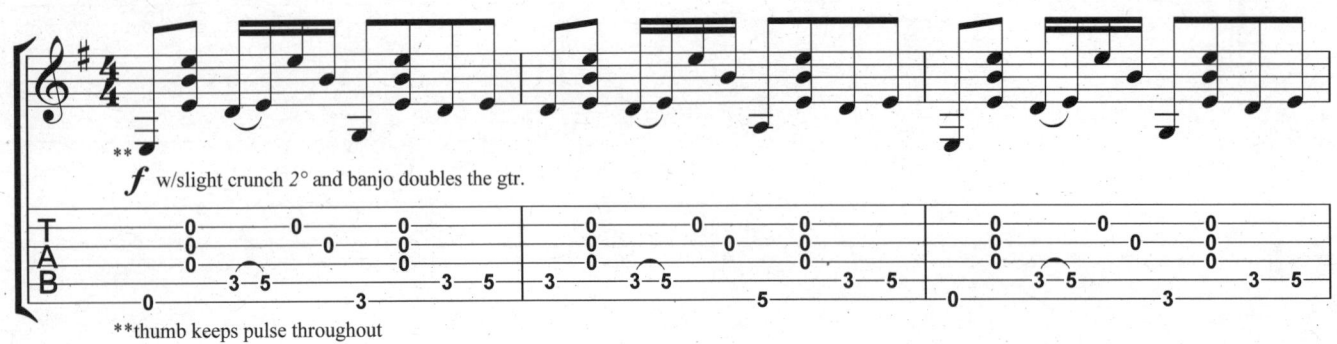

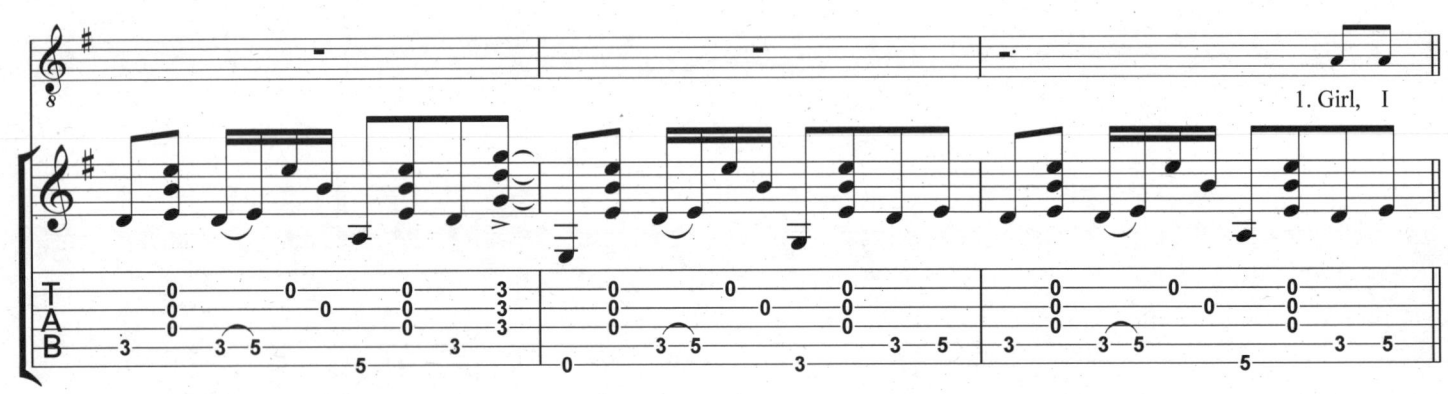

f w/slight crunch 2° and banjo doubles the gtr.

**thumb keeps pulse throughout
Tab 0 = Capo 4th Fret

Verse

don't want to ar- gue, I don't wan- na fight.
are my queen and there ain't no doubt about
turn the lights down low, put the stereo on.

mf 1° acoustic only, cut dist.
2° w/banjo

© COPYRIGHT 2007 FAMILY MUSIC PROPRIETARY LIMITED.
ALL RIGHTS RESERVED. INTERNATIONAL COPYRIGHT SECURED.

it. And if there's
it. And if you
Put on our

some-thing wrong, yes you know I'm gon-na try to make it
want I'll tell the world, yes you know I'll shout
fav-'rite record by Ell-la Fitz' and Lou-is Arm-

right. I love you, you love me, we be
it. The way you walk, talk, move, yeah
-strong. And take you to our living-room dance-

one fam-i-ly to-night. So get right
girl, get me high as a kite. So get right
-floor and I'll hold you tight. I gua-ran-

To Coda
ov - er here and let's get down col' fun - ky (to-)night.
ov - er here and let's get down col' fun - ky (to-)night.
-tee you me gon - na get down fun - ky to - night.
1.
2.
2. Oh, girl you
To - night. What's your name?
w/added crunch dist.
Chorus
Let's go back to when we first met, back in
etc.
f
* bring out lower notes
nine - teen nine - ty nine. 'Prec - i - ate,
TAB

be-fore you knew I was yours___ and you mine,_____ yeah.

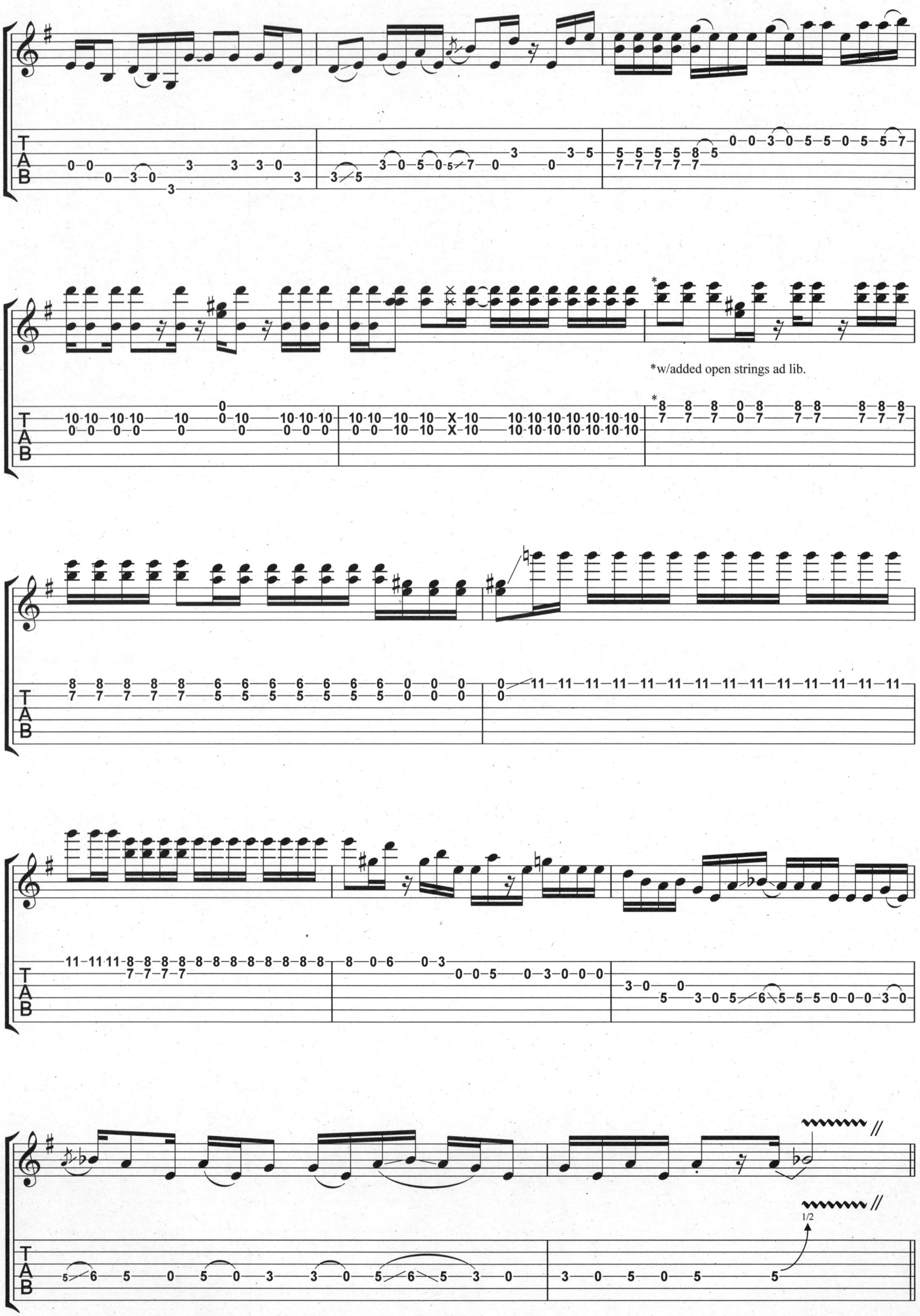
*w/added open strings ad lib.
1/2

25

- na get fun - ky to - night. What's your name?
w/added crunch dist
Chorus
Let's go back to when we first met, back in
etc.
* bring out lower notes
nine - teen nine - ty nine. 'Prec - i - ate, before you
knew I was yours and I knew you were mine. What's your name?

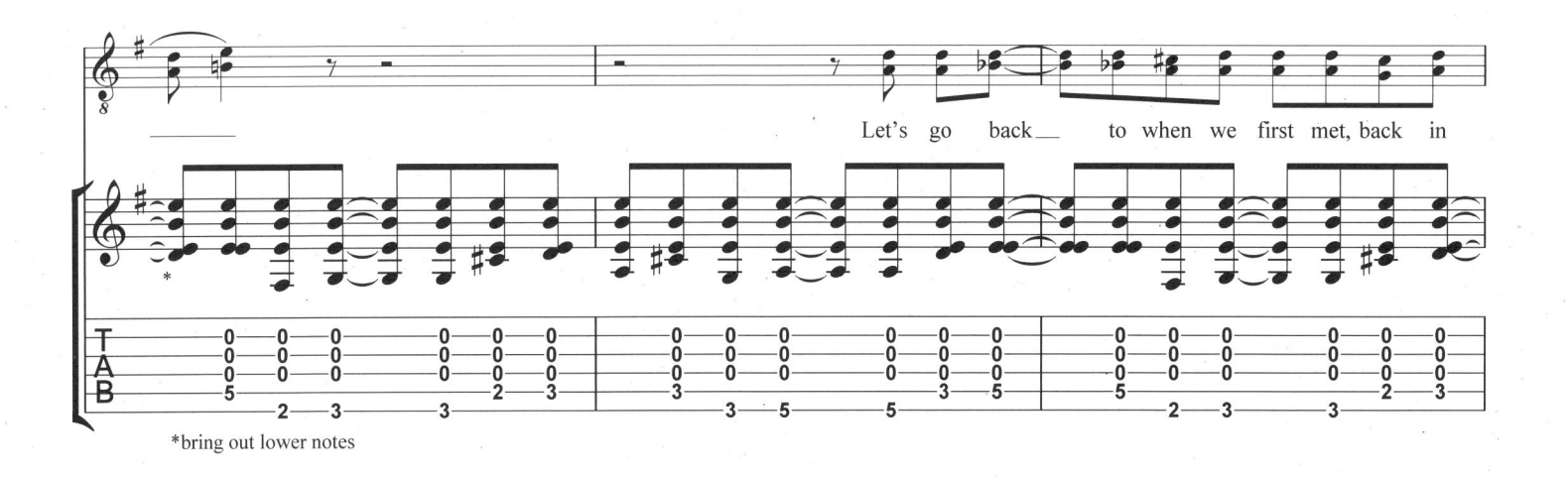

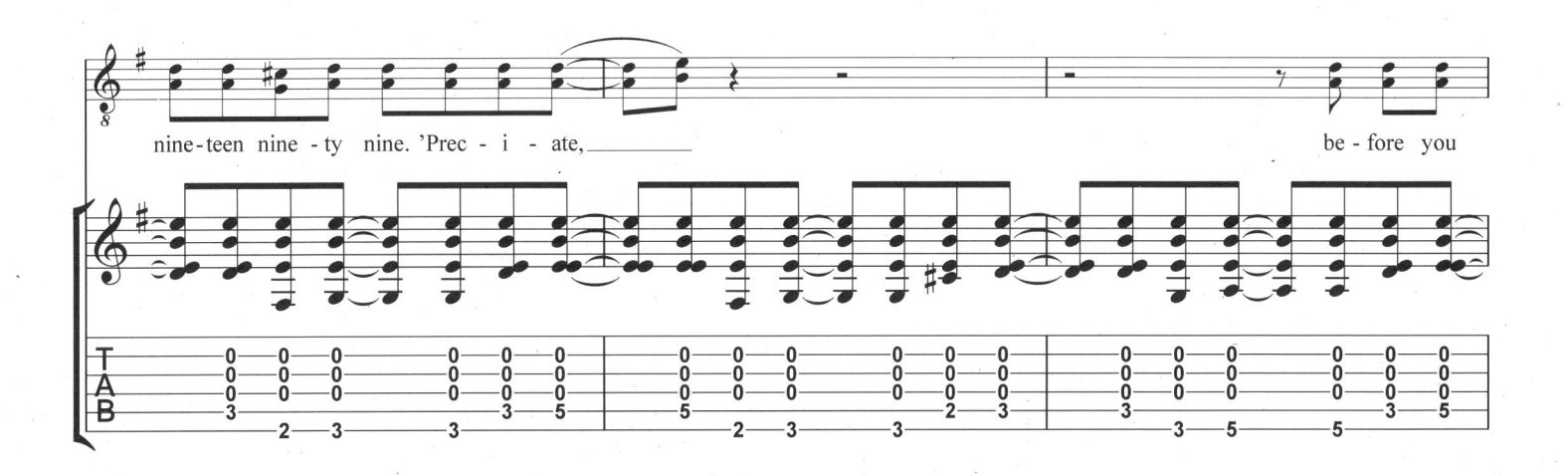

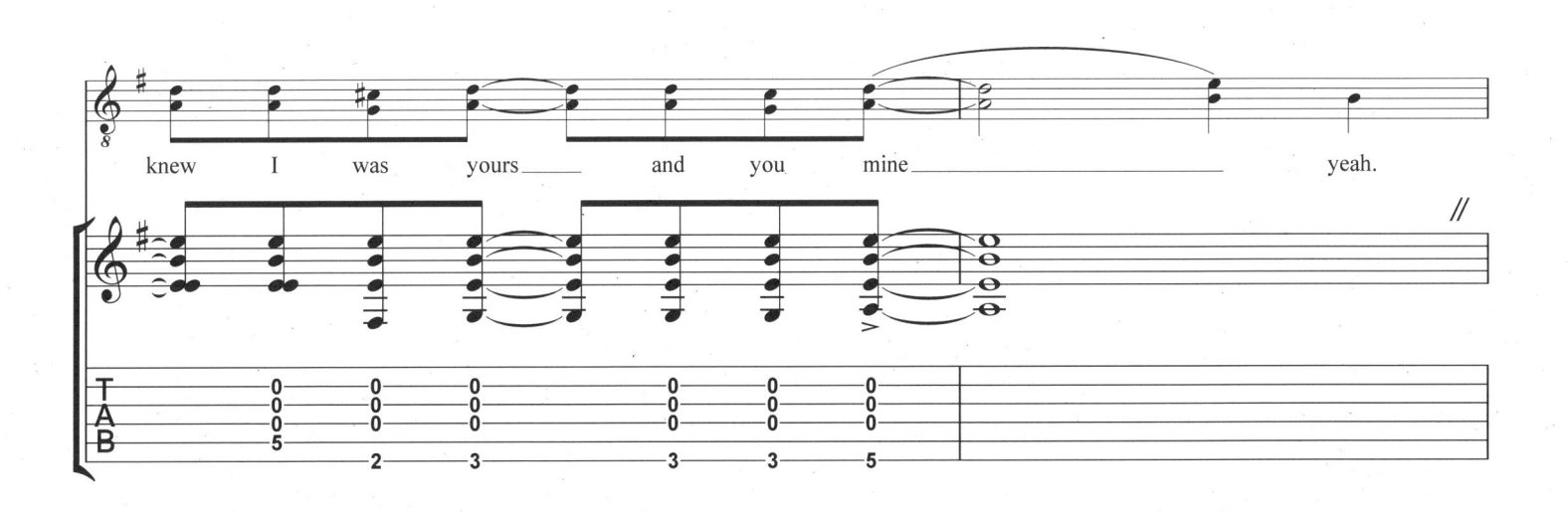

*bring out lower notes

Let's go back to when we first met, back in nine-teen nine-ty nine. 'Prec-i-ate, be-fore you knew I was yours and you mine yeah.

Outro
Bass arr. for Gtr.

Play 4 times

ad lib. on repeats
ad lib. percussive guitar

Gtr. 1
mf-f acoustic only, cut dist.
Play 4 times
Harmonica solo
ff w/octave fx
1, 3, 5.
2.
4.
6.
rit.

CAROLINE

WORDS & MUSIC BY JOHN BUTLER

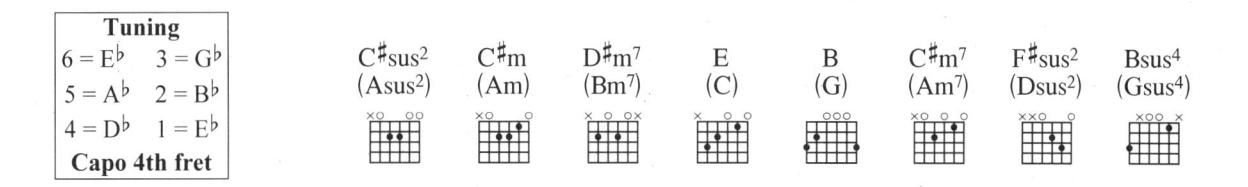

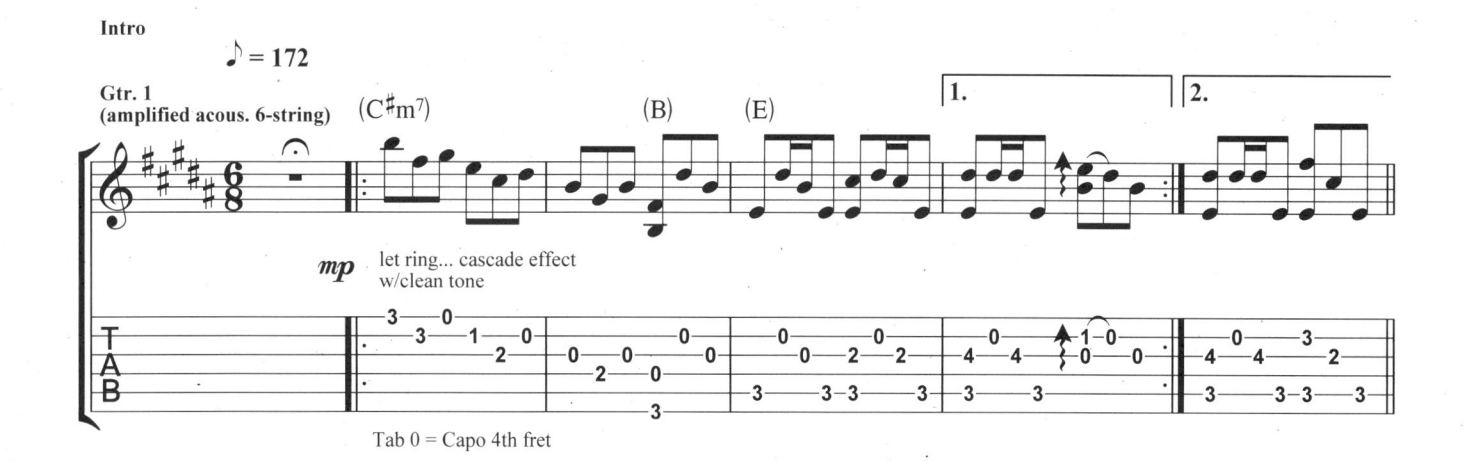

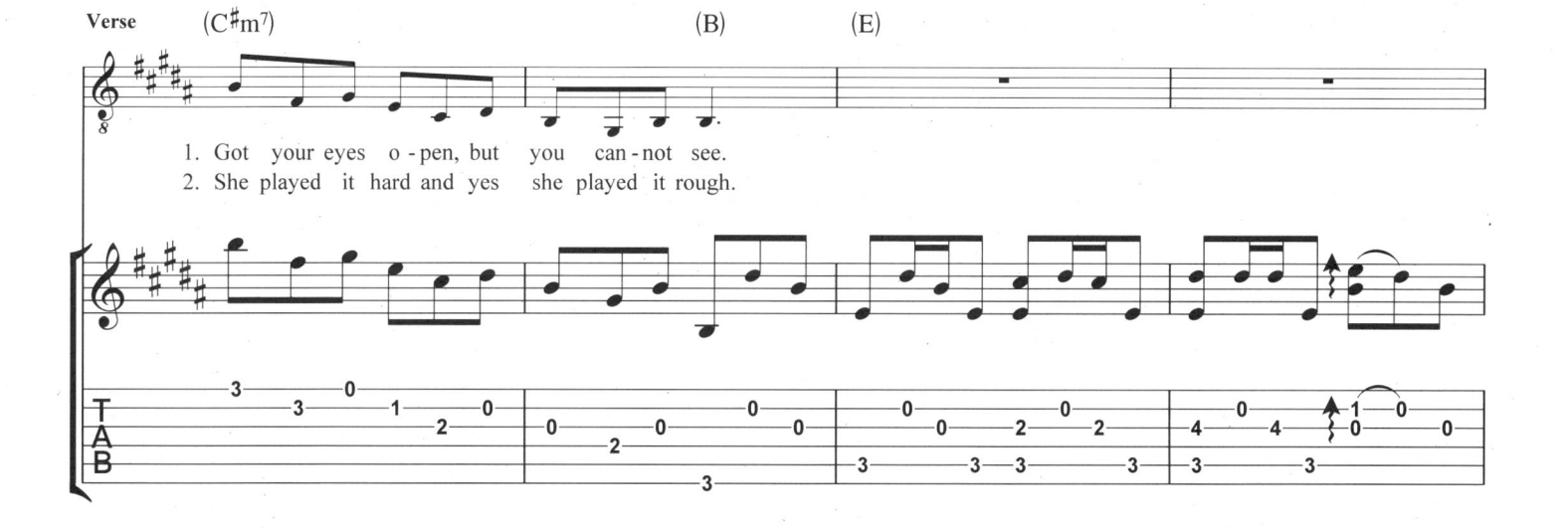

(C#m7) (B) (E)

one day you see some-thing you can-not bear.
rock by rock she built those walls ev-'ry-day.

(C#m7) (B) (E)

Tell-ing you girl, yes you bet-ter be-ware.
Built her-self a tow-er so far a-way. And from

(C#m7) (B) (E)

Her pa-pa loved her so much you could see. I

(C#m7) (B) (E)

loved her too much if you know what I mean. So

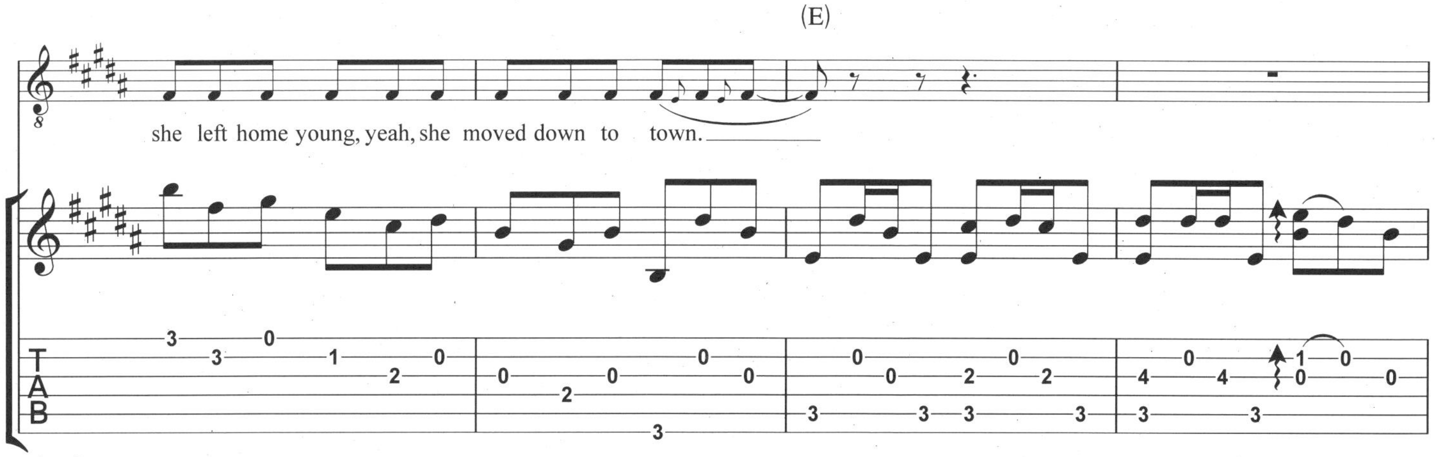

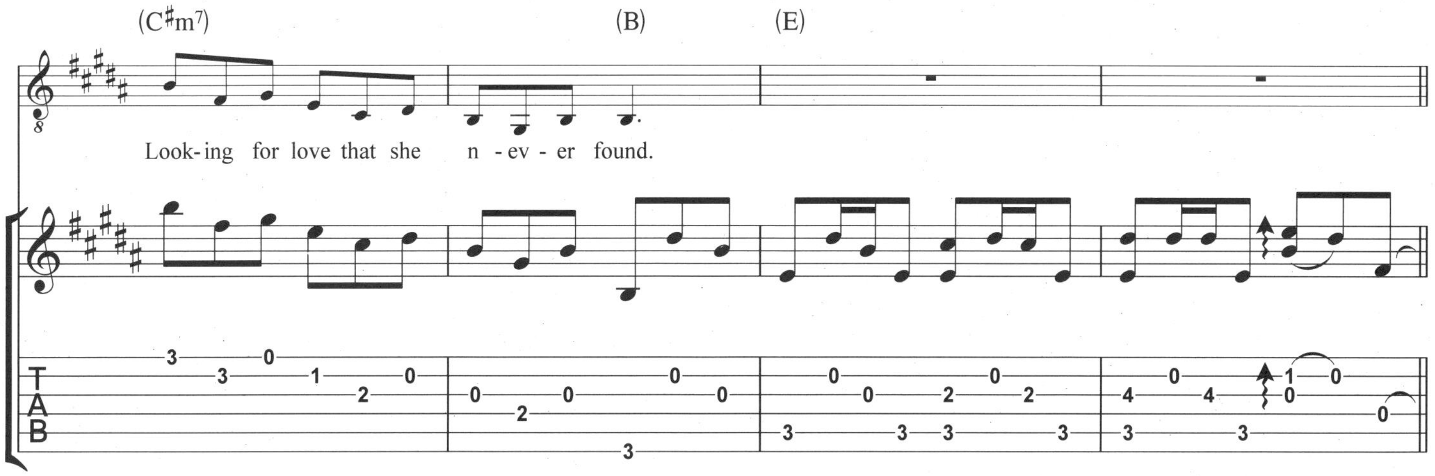

*Symbols in parentheses represent chord names with respect to capoed guitar (TAB 0 = 4th fret). Symbols above represent actual sounding chords.

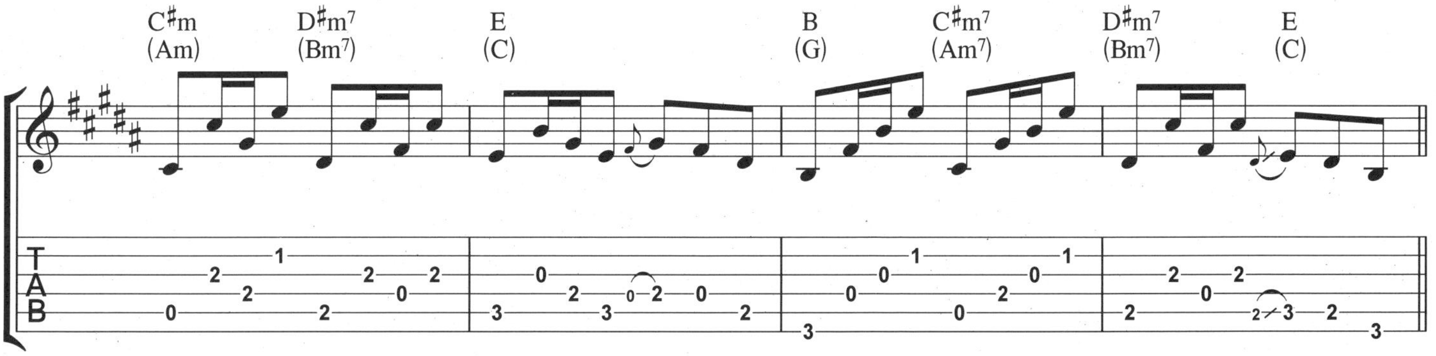

Verse
(C♯m7)
(B)
(E)
2. She played it hard and yes she played it rough.
(C♯m7)
(B)
(E)
Made her feel safe and it made her feel tough. And
(C♯m7)
(B)
(E)
rock by rock she built those walls ev - 'ry - day.
(C♯m7)
(B)
(E)
Built her - self a tow - er so far a - way. And from

Bridge

birds could fly high high in over their castle she knew
up in that troubles she gonna

no-one could get too close to touch. And if
find some of her own wings and fly. And no-

life and death were such a game why did
-one could convince or pay her double or tell her

they all make such a fuss?
she was too young to die. Oh,

34

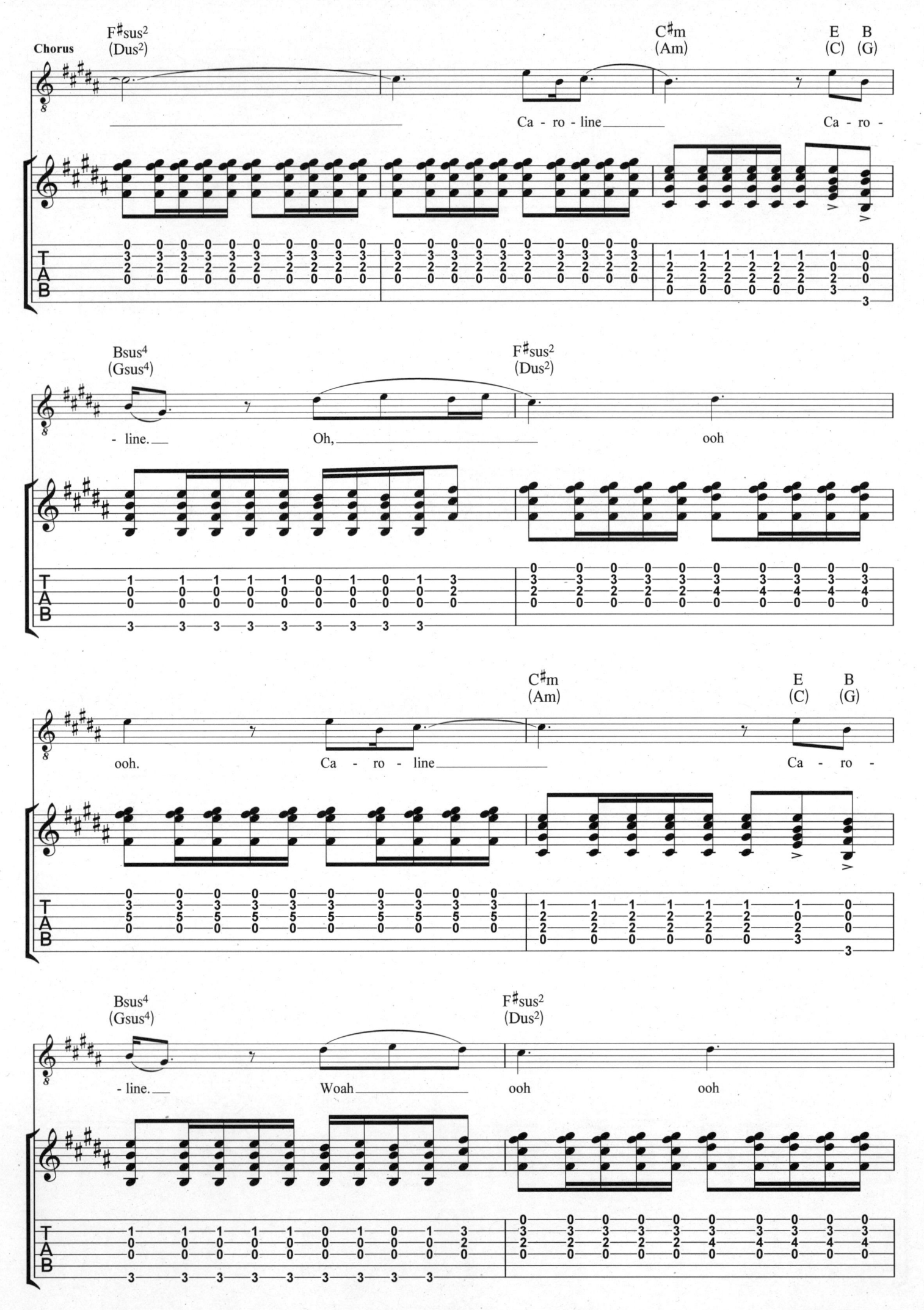

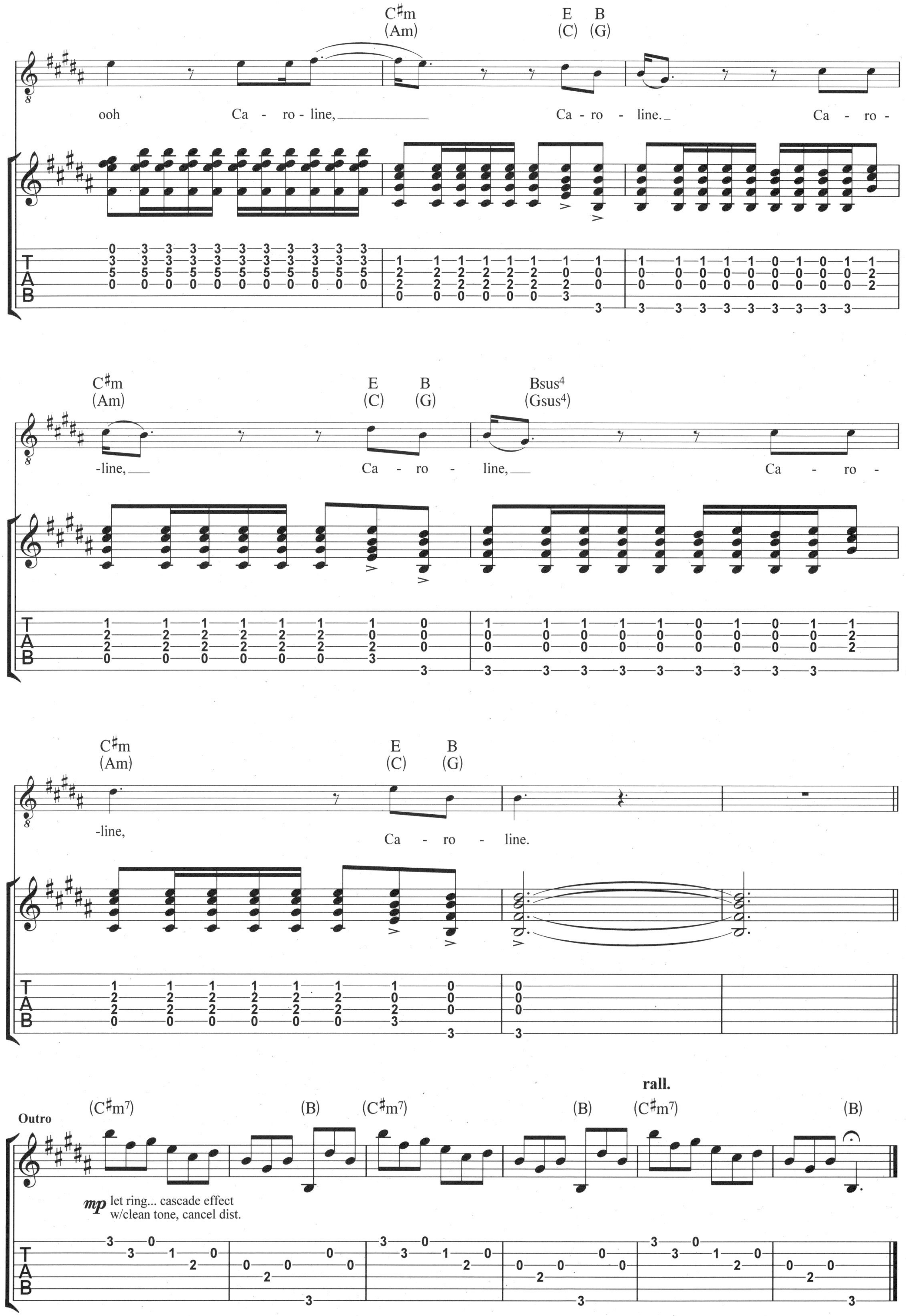
C♯m (Am)
E (C) B (G)
ooh Ca - ro - line,
Ca - ro - line.
Ca - ro -
C♯m (Am)
E (C) B (G)
Bsus4 (Gsus4)
-line,
Ca - ro - line,
Ca - ro -
C♯m (Am)
E (C) B (G)
-line,
Ca - ro - line.
Outro
rall.
(C♯m7) (B) (C♯m7) (B) (C♯m7) (B)
mp let ring... cascade effect
w/clean tone, cancel dist.

GOOD EXCUSE

WORDS & MUSIC BY JOHN BUTLER

© COPYRIGHT 2007 FAMILY MUSIC PROPRIETARY LIMITED.
ALL RIGHTS RESERVED. INTERNATIONAL COPYRIGHT SECURED.

A G A G
things don't seem to go my way.
I really got a good excuse to com - plain. My parents got divorced, can't heal the pain.
A G A G
Got a dark cloud that's hang - ing,
And now there is only cheap regrets
A G A G
and it seems to fol - low me.
I guess that's just the way it be. Is it the world or how I see
tacet 2°
A G A G
Boy, won't you just wake up (and) feel the hum - ming
me? Boy, now you are real - ly, real - ly bug - gin',
Gtrs. 1+2 (amplified 6 string acous.)
mf
cont. in slashes

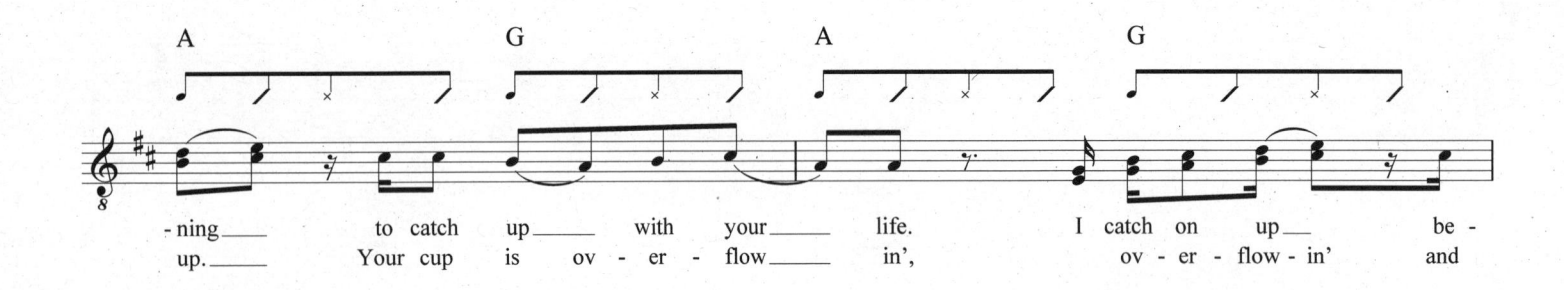

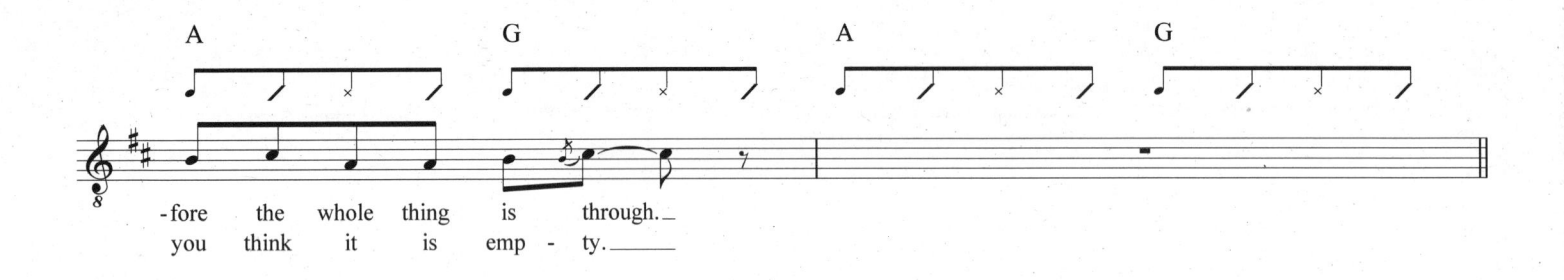

| A | G | A | G |

this good world is giv-ing you. I bet-ter start run-
yes you are bug-gin' me. Can you just shut right

| A | G | A | G |

-ning to catch up with your life. I catch on up be-
up. Your cup is ov-er-flow-in', ov-er-flow-in' and

| A | G | A | G |

-fore the whole thing is through.
you think it is emp-ty.

Verse

| A | G | A | G |

3. Have you once, have you twice, have you ev-en con-ceived how
4. You don't even know what side you are fight-ing for

| A | G | A | G |

real-ly good boy you do got it, go take an-oth-er bet-ter look a-round.
boy, won't you turn your Gameboy off, stop pre-tend-ing it's you a-gainst the world.

| A | G | A | G |

You are just an-oth-er white boy think-ing you're so hard.
I am sick and I am tired of hearing you al-ways say

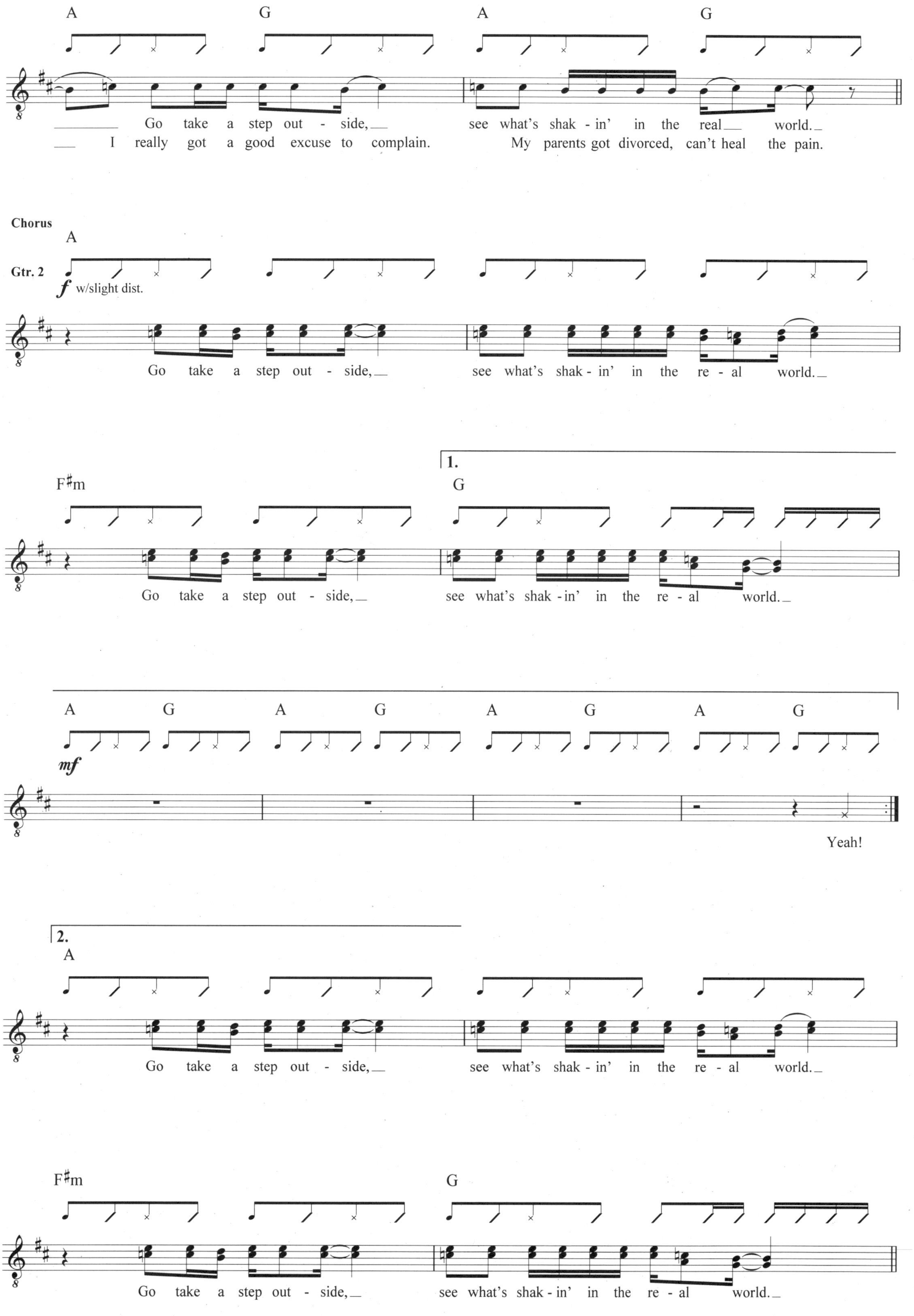
A G A G
Go take a step out - side, see what's shak - in' in the real world.
I really got a good excuse to complain. My parents got divorced, can't heal the pain.
Chorus
A
Gtr. 2
f w/slight dist.
Go take a step out - side, see what's shak - in' in the re - al world.
F♯m
1.
G
Go take a step out - side, see what's shak - in' in the re - al world.
A G A G A G A G
mf
Yeah!
2.
A
Go take a step out - side, see what's shak - in' in the re - al world.
F♯m
G
Go take a step out - side, see what's shak - in' in the re - al world.

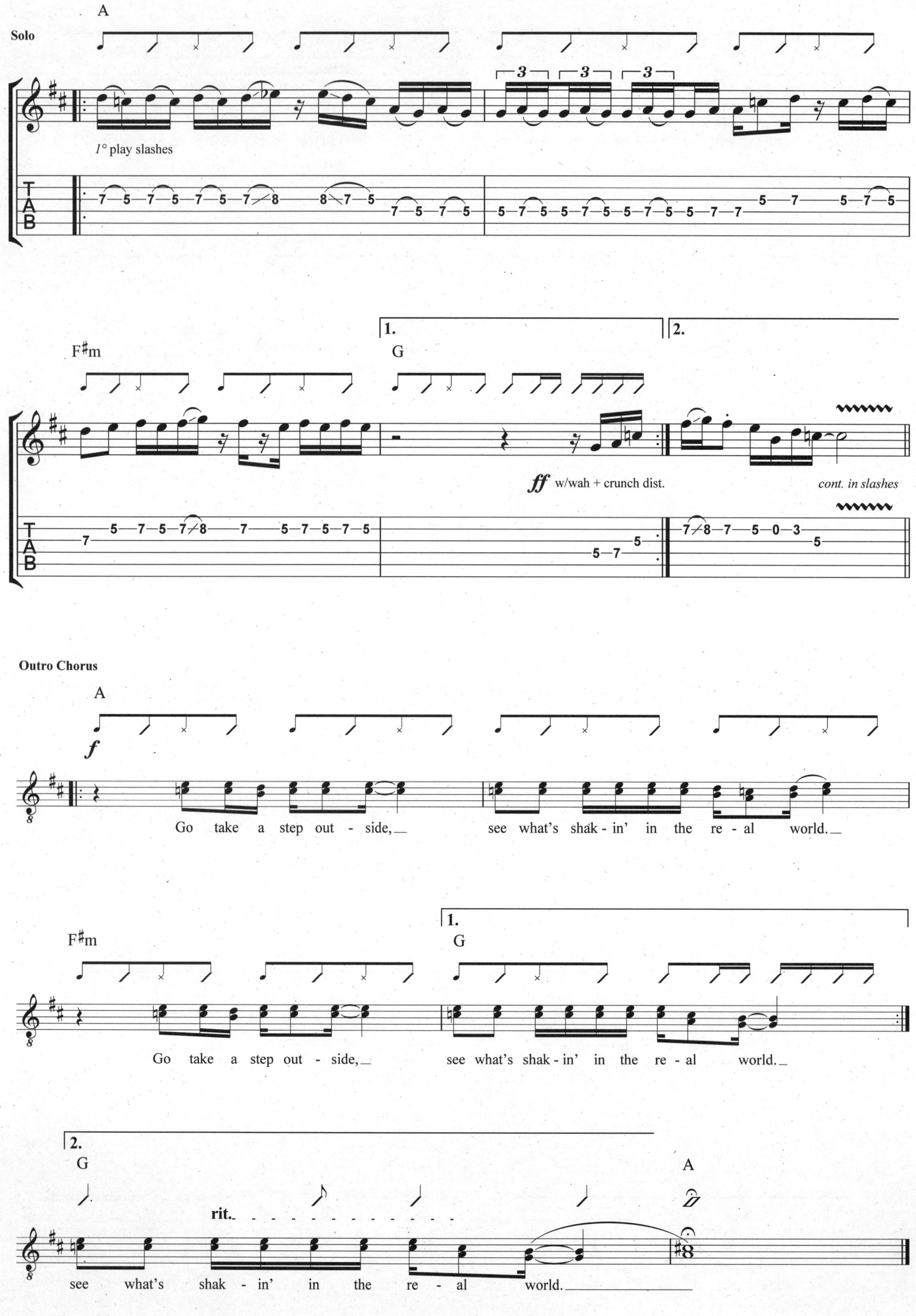
Solo
A
1° play slashes
F♯m
1.
G
2.
ff w/wah + crunch dist.
cont. in slashes
Outro Chorus
A
f
Go take a step out - side,
see what's shak - in' in the re - al world.
F♯m
1.
G
Go take a step out - side,
see what's shak - in' in the re - al world.
2.
G
A
rit.
see what's shak - in' in the re - al world.

DEVIL RUNNING

WORDS & MUSIC BY JOHN BUTLER

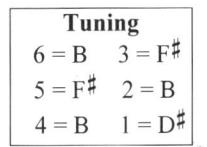

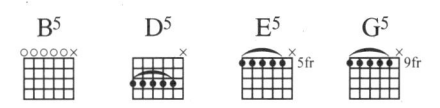

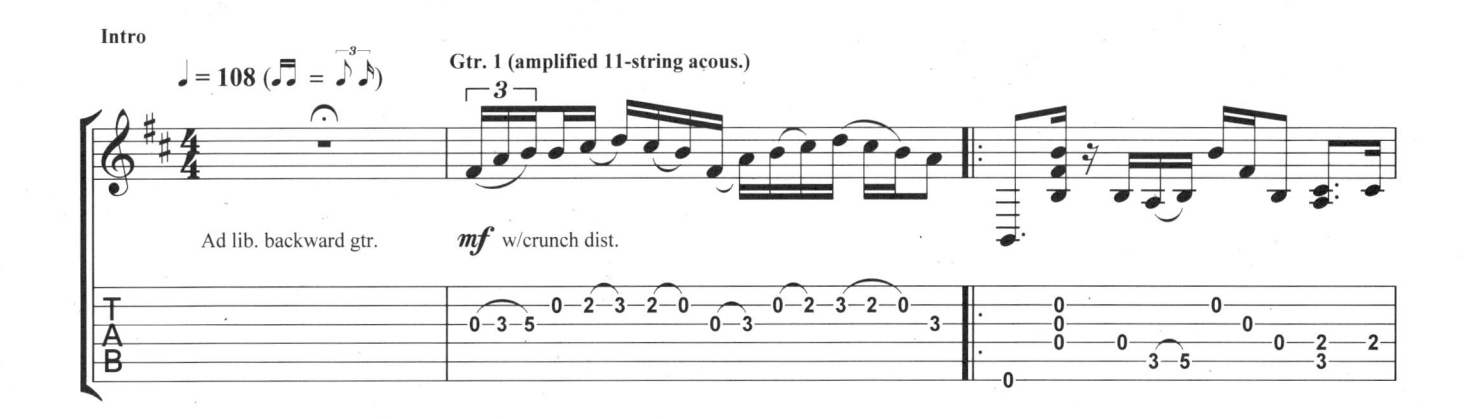

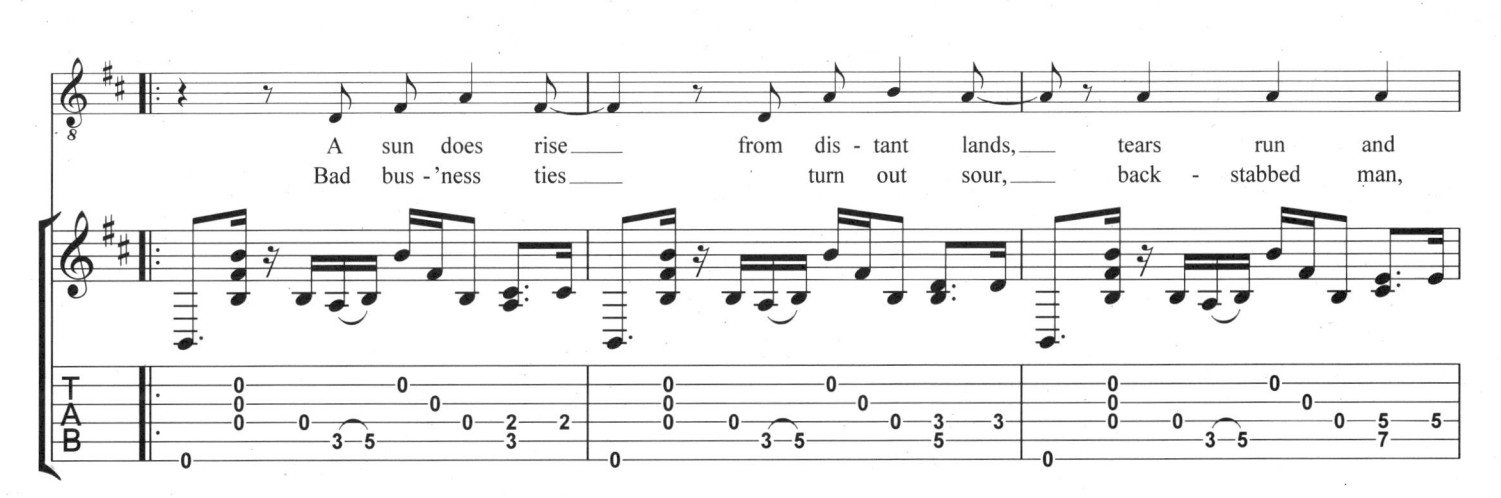

fi - res burn - ing. He finds first place,___ with dir - ty hands
no - thing for - got - ten. And in an un - for - got - ten hour___

___ he gra - du - ates man with - out learn - ing. A - gen - da set___
___ seeds___ fall from an ap - ple rot - ten. Now hate and fear___

so long a - go___ this one's a pup - pet with a mas - ter.
have their own way___ and don't the scum just love the dis - trac - tion.

The hands stand still___ right by his side,___
Black blood will need___ to be lanced___

_____ middle finger on the button of disaster.
_____ and when it's found you just blamed____ the guilty faction.

Chorus

And most of us____ we stand and watch like old lady getting
And now it's time____ not just to watch like old lady getting

handbag stolen. It's time to chase,____ chase them criminals. Lord,____
handbag stolen. It's time to chase,____ chase them criminals. Lord,____

____ I see the Devil and the Devil is running.____
____ I see the Devil and the Devil is running.____

43

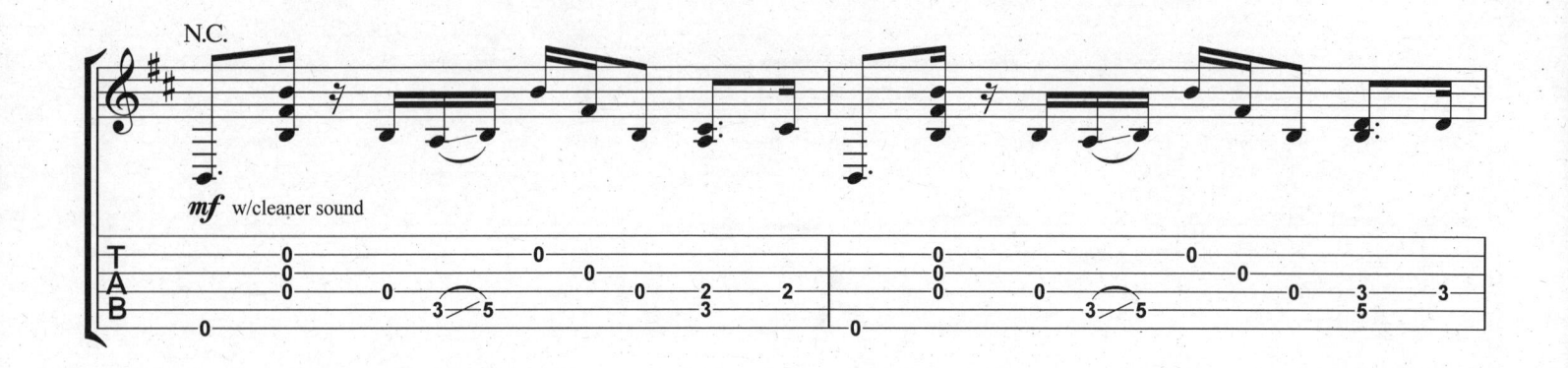

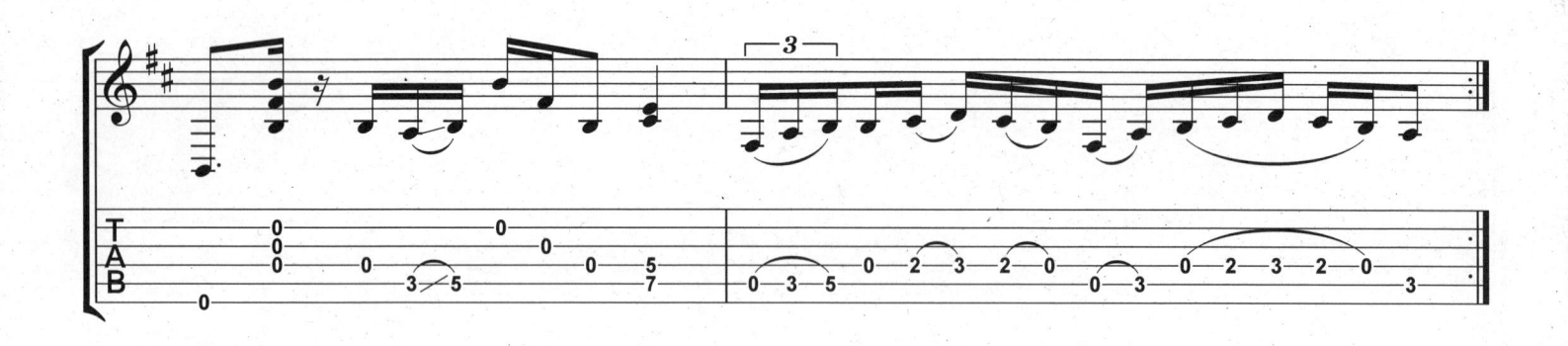

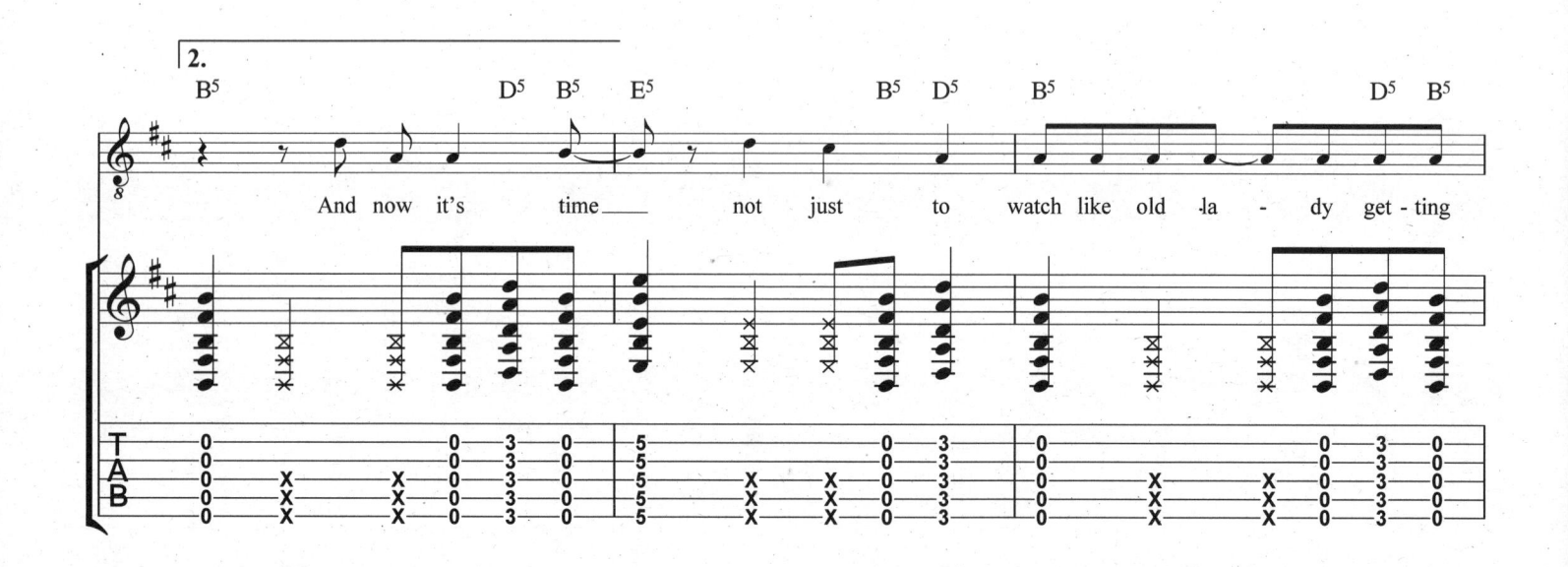

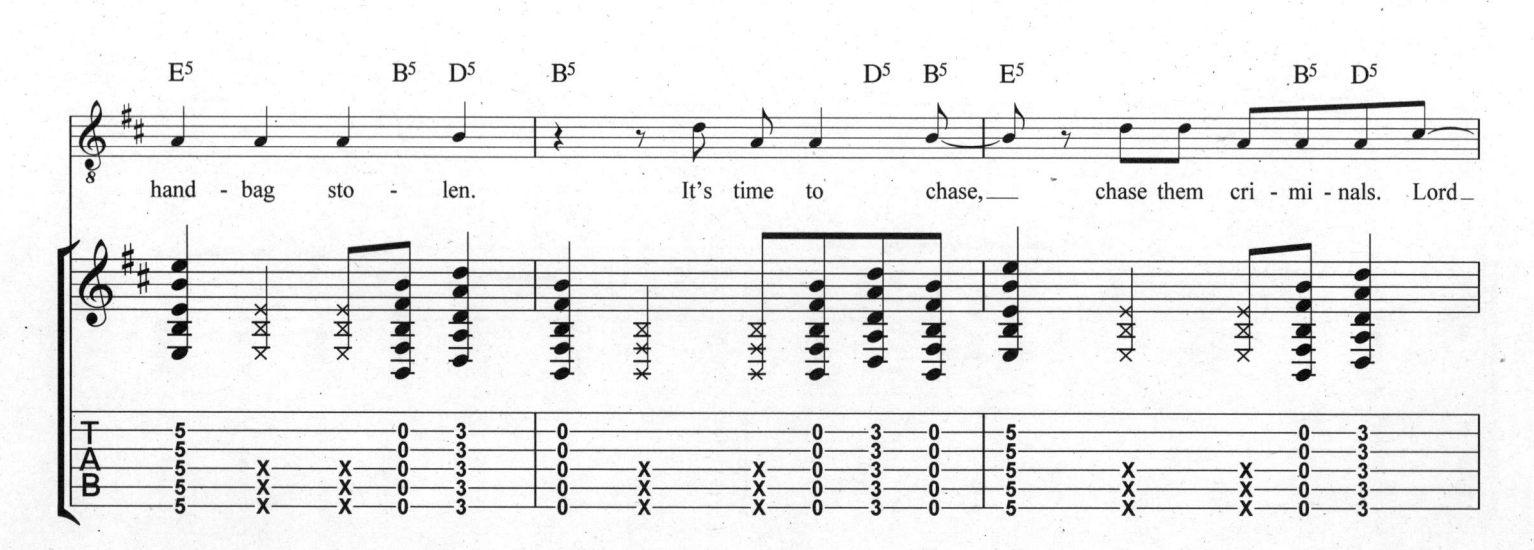

And now it's time___ not just to watch like old la-dy get-ting hand-bag sto-len. It's time to chase,___ chase them cri-mi-nals. Lord___

B5
D5 B5
E5
D5
I see the De - vil and the Dev - il is run - ning.
let ring...
(ad lib. vocal)
E5
G5
(Eeh - Oh)
let ring...
let ring...
A5
Solo
B5
w/wah
rake

46

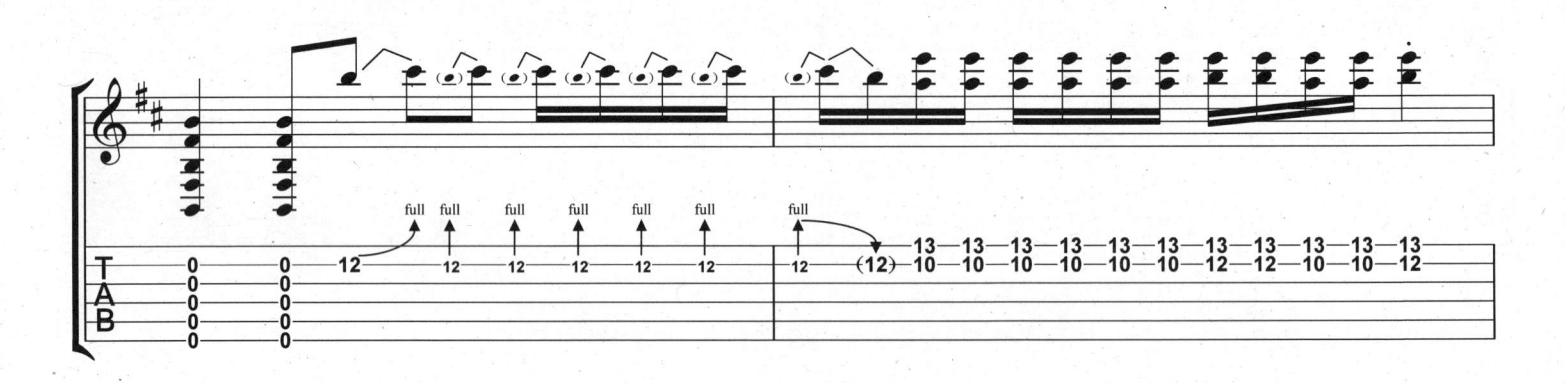

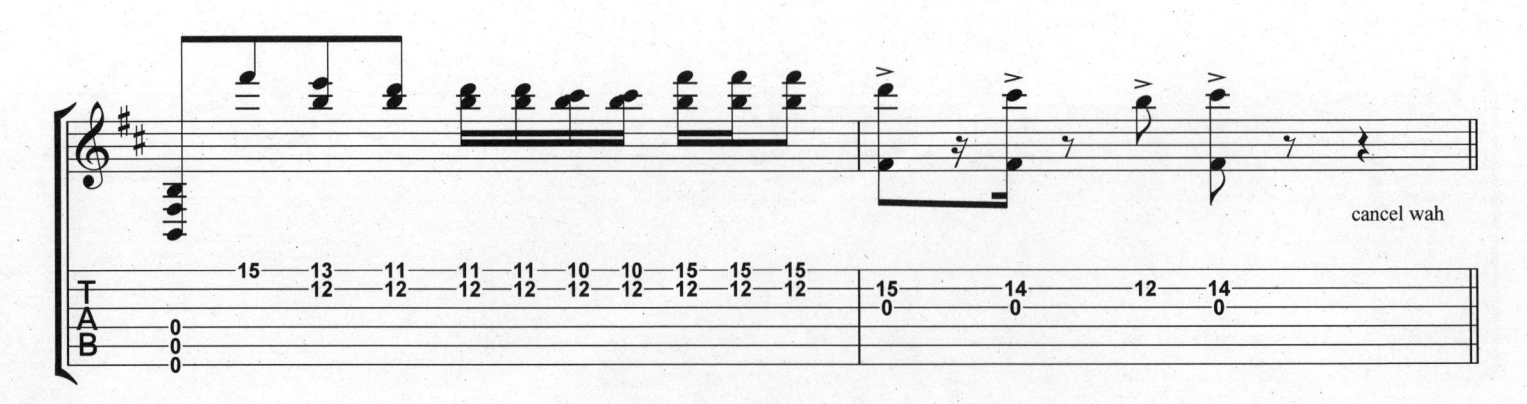

Outro Chorus

And now it's time___ not just to watch like old lady getting hand-bag sto-len. It's time to chase,___ chase them cri-mi-nals. Lord___ I see the De-vil and the De-vil is run-ing.

Dev-il is run-ing.

LOSING YOU

WORDS & MUSIC BY JOHN BUTLER

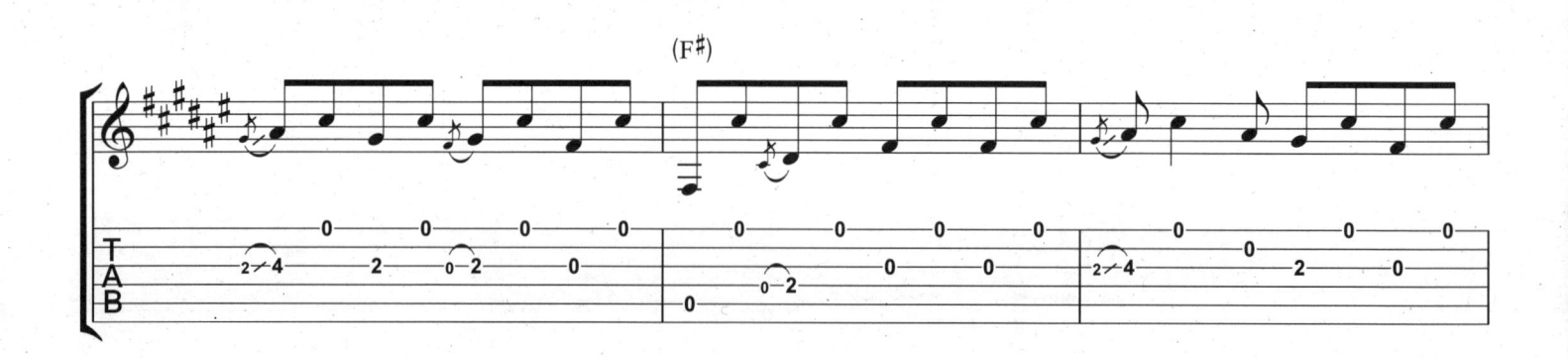

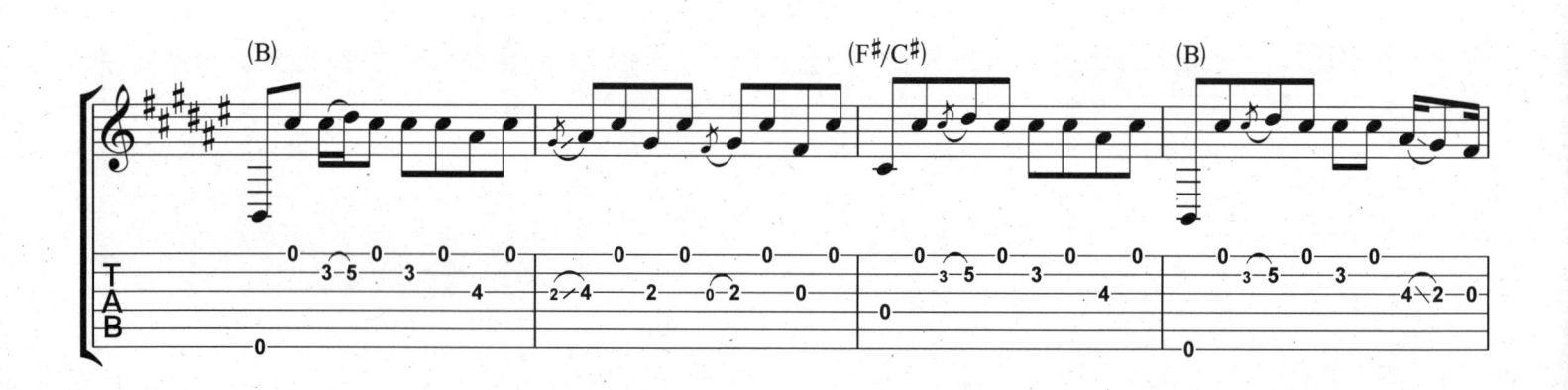

G tuning with low C down a step
6 = B   3 = F#
5 = F#   2 = A#
4 = C#   1 = C#

Intro
♩ = 138
Gtr. 1 (Tri-cone Resonator)

© COPYRIGHT 2007 FAMILY MUSIC PROPRIETARY LIMITED.
ALL RIGHTS RESERVED. INTERNATIONAL COPYRIGHT SECURED.

48

Verse
(F♯)
1.There are things in this life I
(B)
would ra - ther
not sac - ri - fice.
(F♯)
You girl, I can - not live with - out
(B)
and you know
there's no doubt that
(F♯/C♯)
all I mind's
(B)
los - ing
(F♯)
you.
To Coda

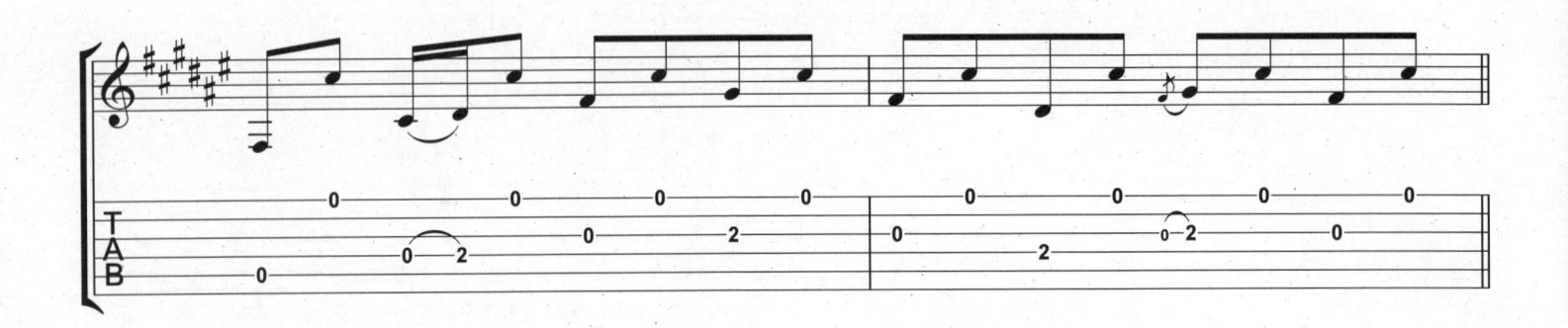

Verse

2. And I don't mind losing sleep, pray the Lord my soul to keep. I'll get plenty rest when I am dead but, ah 'til then won't you share my bed. 'Cos all I mind's

3. And I don't mind losing money, there's nothing this life owes me. I've been given more than I can receive but for, for you there is no receipt. So

50

losing you.

All I mind's losing you.

you. Oh.

51

4. And I don't mind growing old, losing teeth and

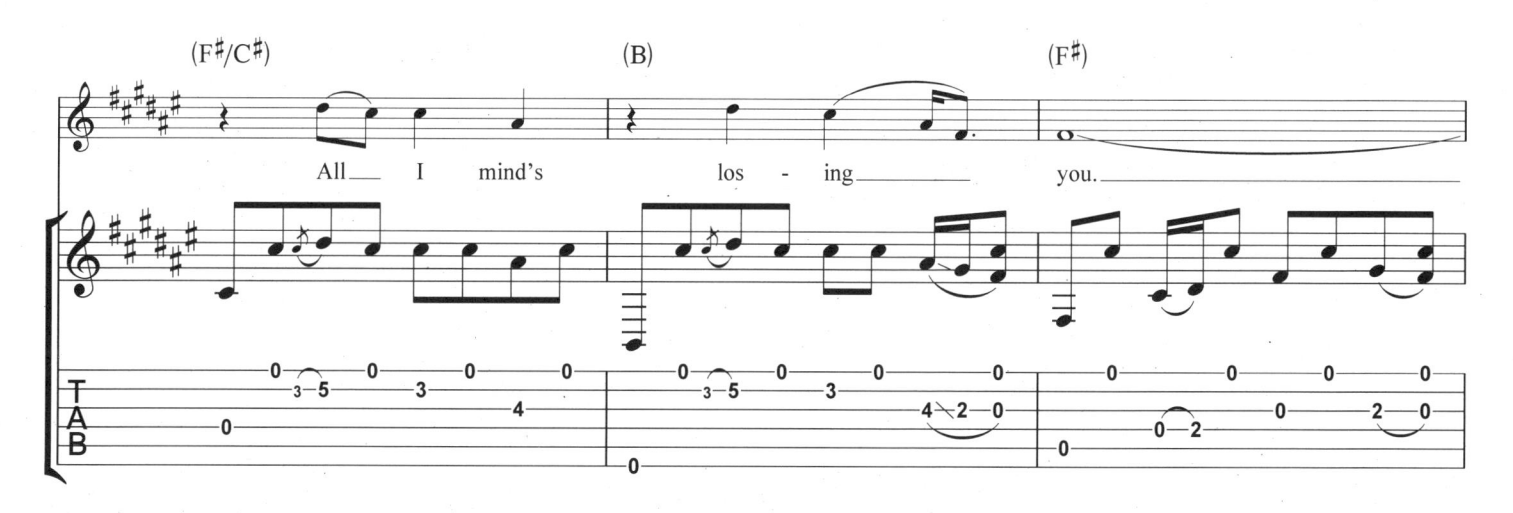

growing bald. Not as handsome as I never was but you love me just be-cause all I mind's los-ing you. All I mind's los-ing you.

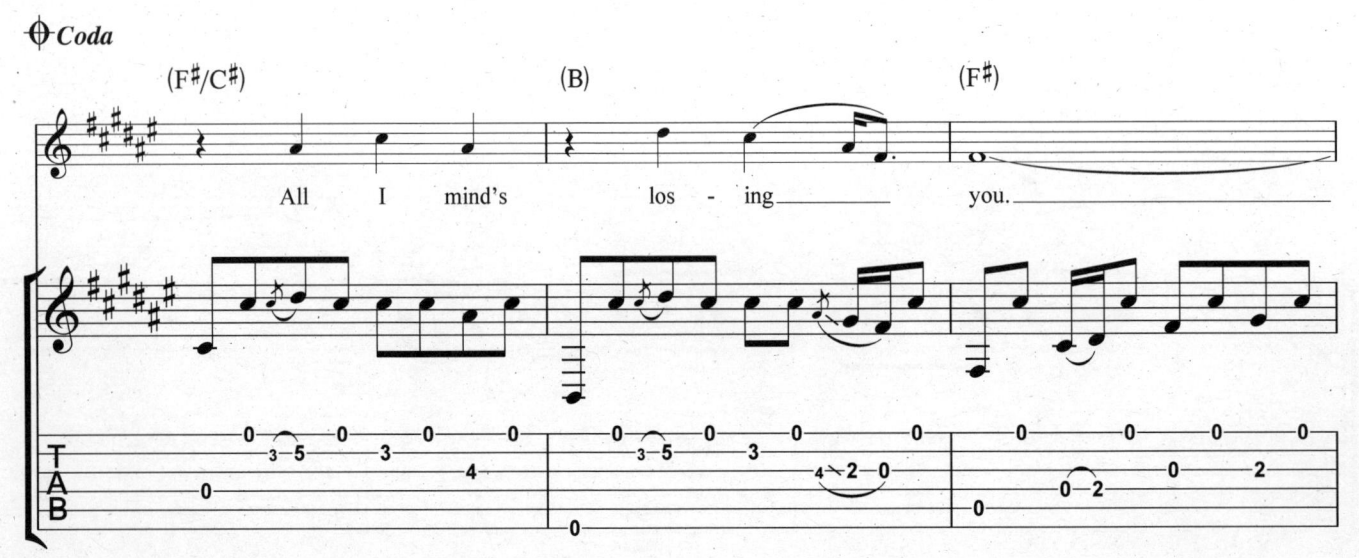

D.S. al Coda

Coda

(F#/C#) (B) (F#)

All I mind's los - ing you.

All I mind's los - ing you.

FIRE IN THE SKY

WORDS & MUSIC BY JOHN BUTLER

Tuning
6 = B   3 = F#
5 = F# 2 = B
4 = B   1 = C#

Intro

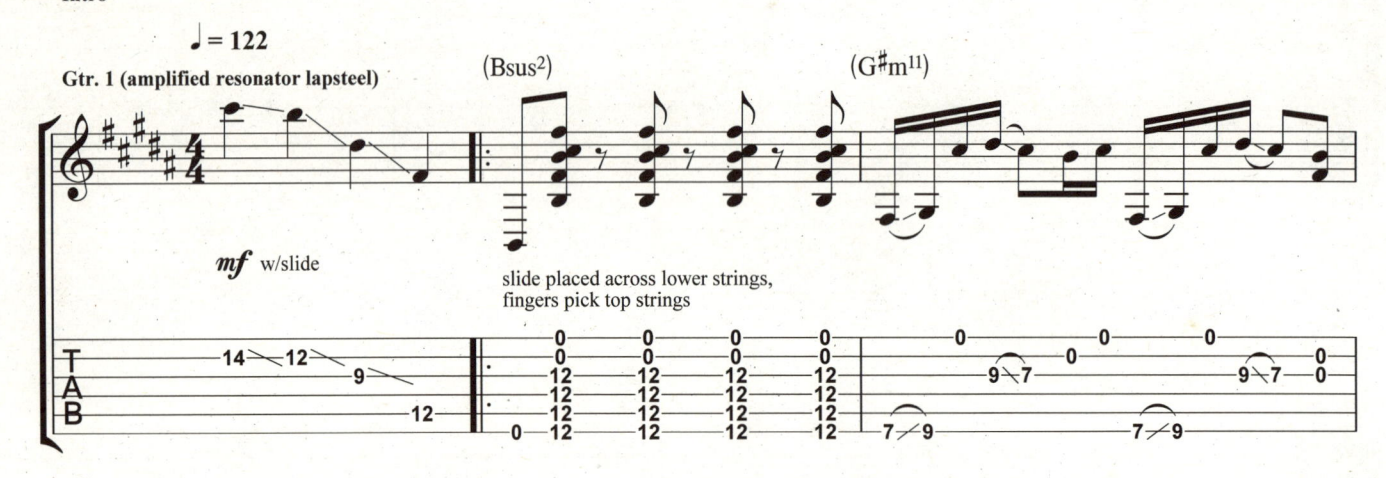

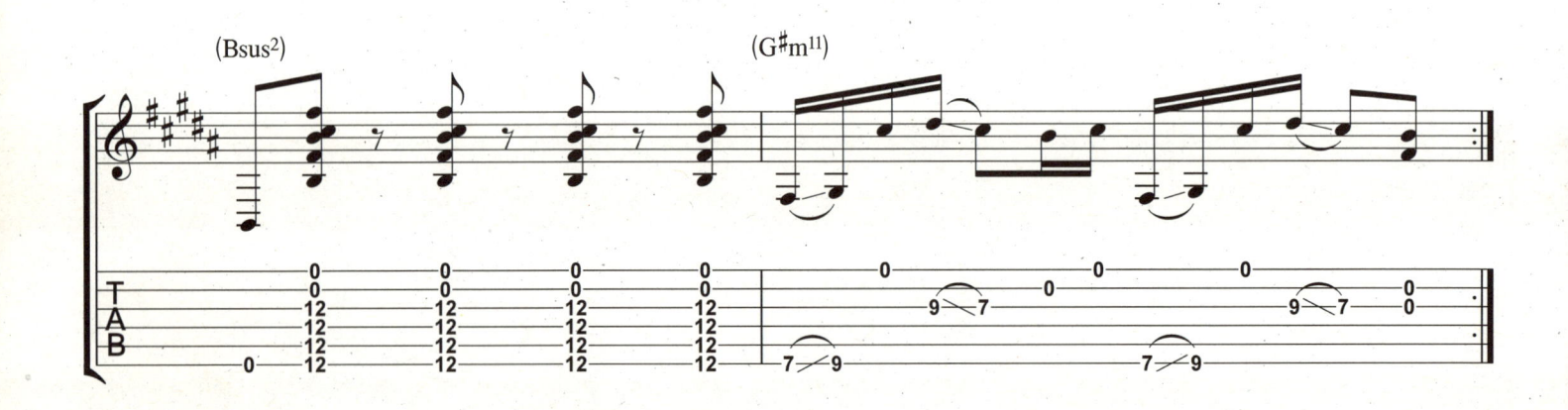

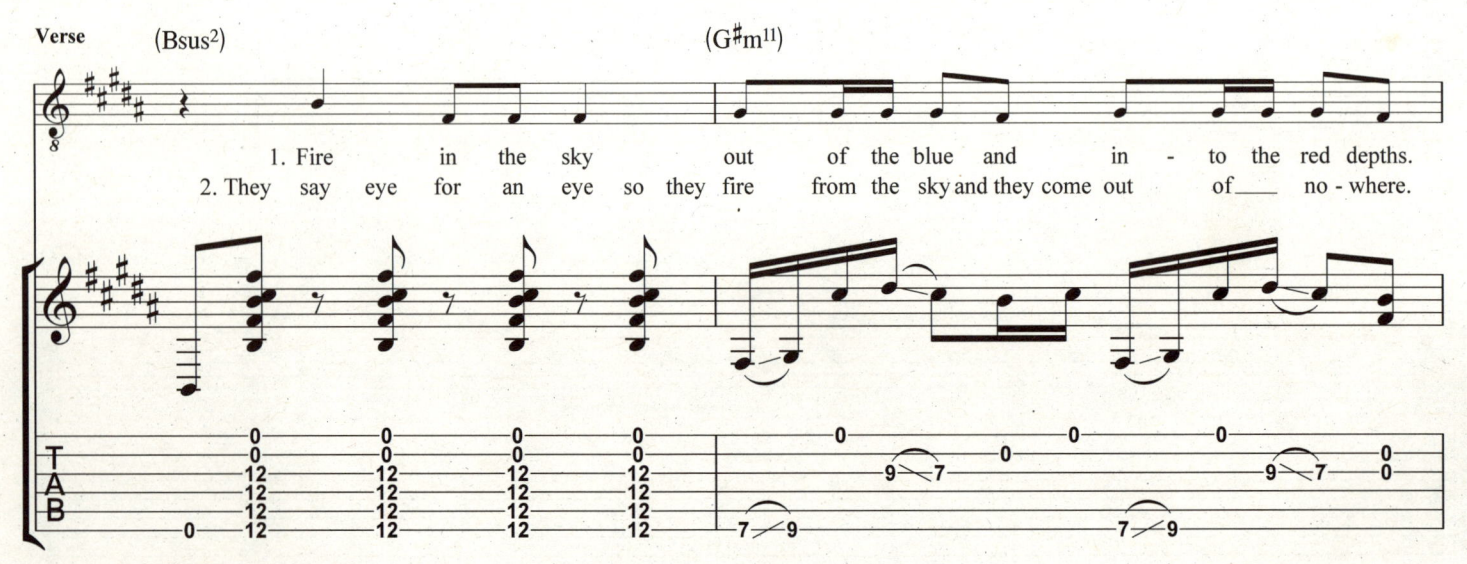

♩ = 122

Gtr. 1 (amplified resonator lapsteel)

(Bsus2)   (G#m11)

mf w/slide

slide placed across lower strings, fingers pick top strings

(Bsus2)   (G#m11)

Verse   (Bsus2)   (G#m11)

1. Fire in the sky out of the blue and in-to the red depths.
2. They say eye for an eye so they fire from the sky and they come out of___ no-where.

© COPYRIGHT 2007 FAMILY MUSIC PROPRIETARY LIMITED.
ALL RIGHTS RESERVED. INTERNATIONAL COPYRIGHT SECURED.

(Bsus²)   (G♯m¹¹)

Time for you and I to try to fall a-sleep in the bed they've made us.
Time for you and I to turn on the big screen and see what's hap-penin'.

(Bsus²)   (G♯m¹¹)

All came crum-blin' down, tears in our eyes as it rained con-fu-sion.
And as those child-ren die pawns in the game of col-later-al dam-age.

(Bsus²)   (G♯m¹¹)

The whole world has changed.
The whole world goes mad.

(Bsus²)   (G♯m¹¹)   (Bsus²)

I don't un-der-stand how one can kill a man.
Stand-ing here on quick-sand a, the more we fight we sink.
Bury the hatch-et deep so we all can weep

Gtrs. 1+2 (acous.)

57

(G#m11) (Bsus2) (G#m11)
In the name of peace
And ven-geance gives us hope,
and heal all this pain so,
1. 2, 3.
(Bsus2) (G#m11) (G#m11)
that's ri-dic-u-lous.
at least that's what we think
so we can live a-gain, so
at least that's what we think. 'Cause
so we can live a-gain. 'Cause
f
Chorus
(E5) (F#5) (G#5)
as we make a-mends by get-ting our re-venge, we sort no-thing out,
Gtr. 1
w/crunch dist.
(F#5) (E5) (F#5)
just add to the doubt. With God on both sides if death is jus-ti-fied,

what - ev - er the name, then we're all to blame.

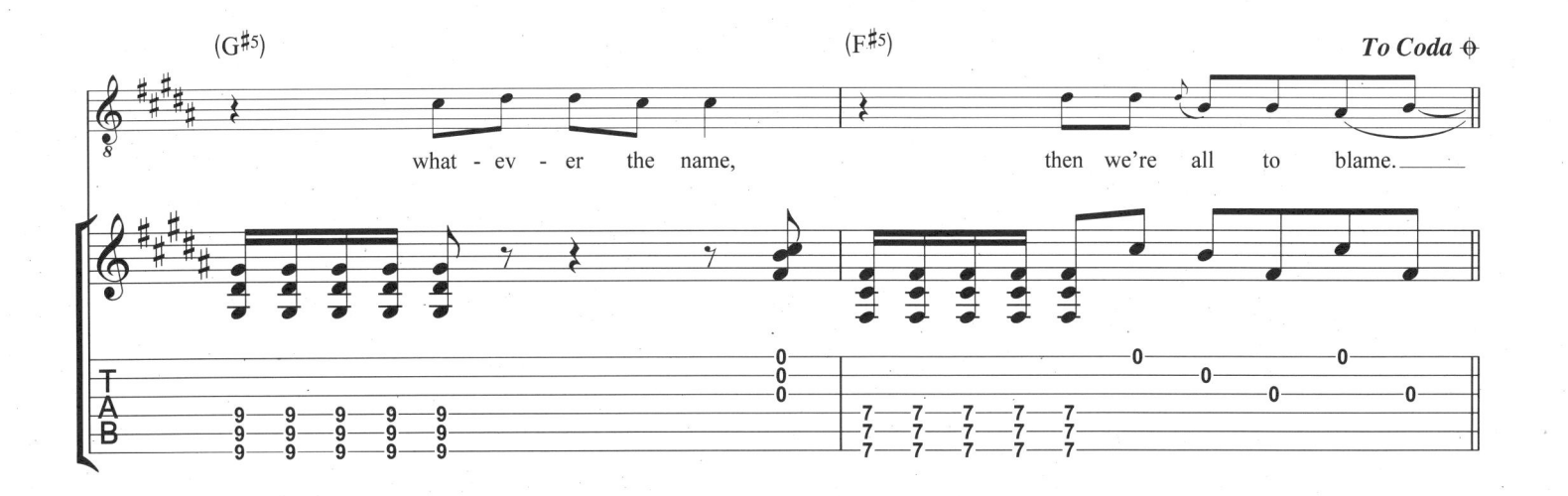

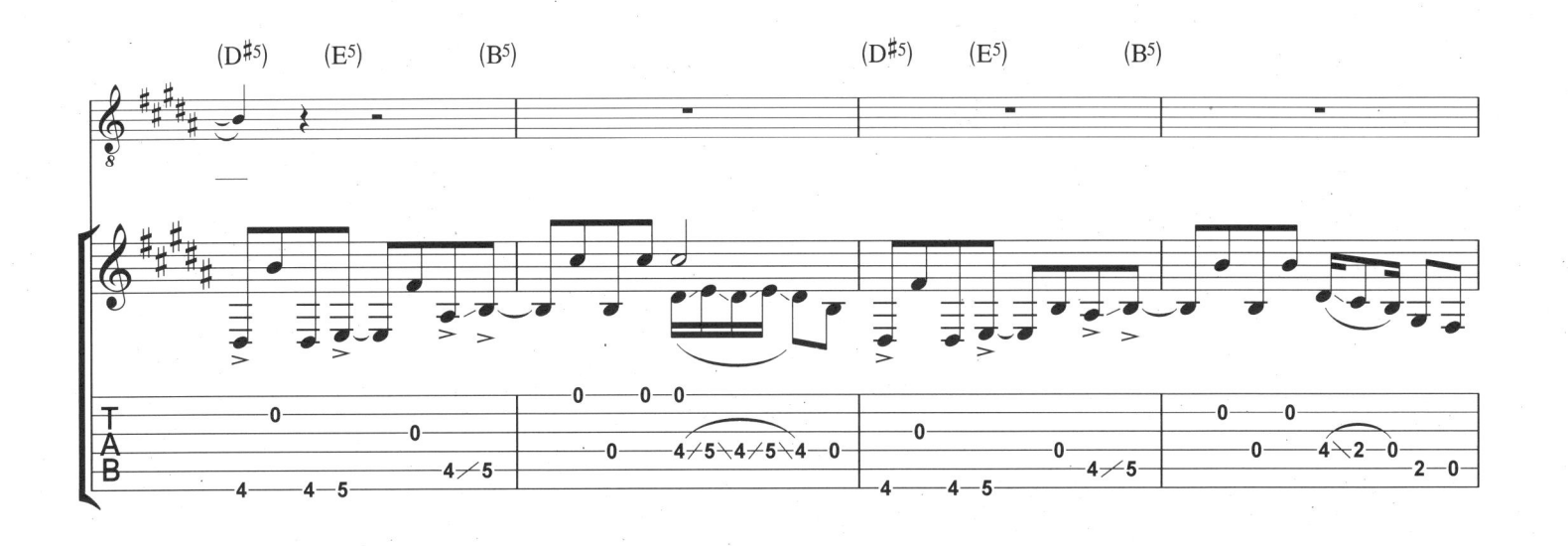

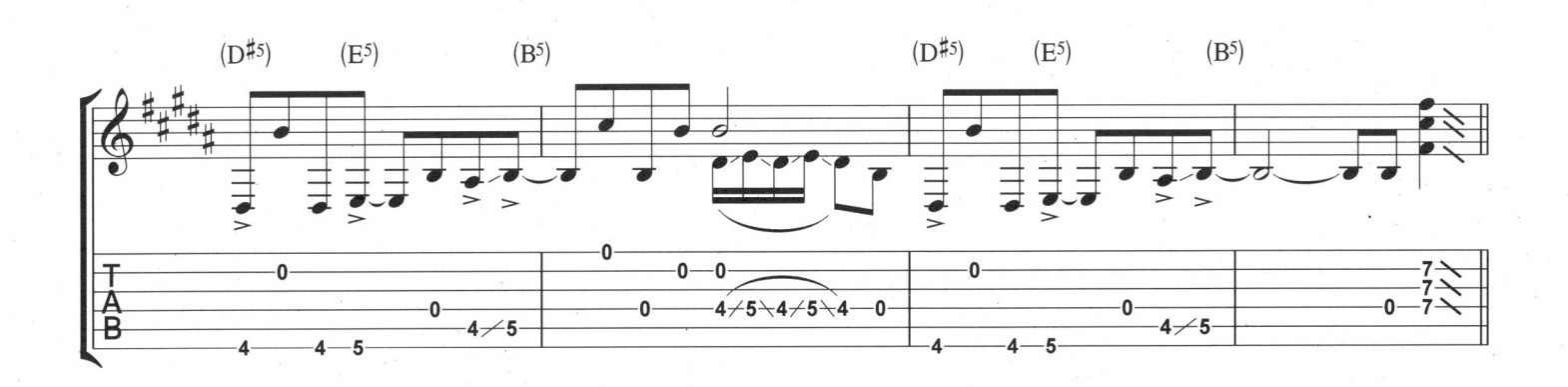

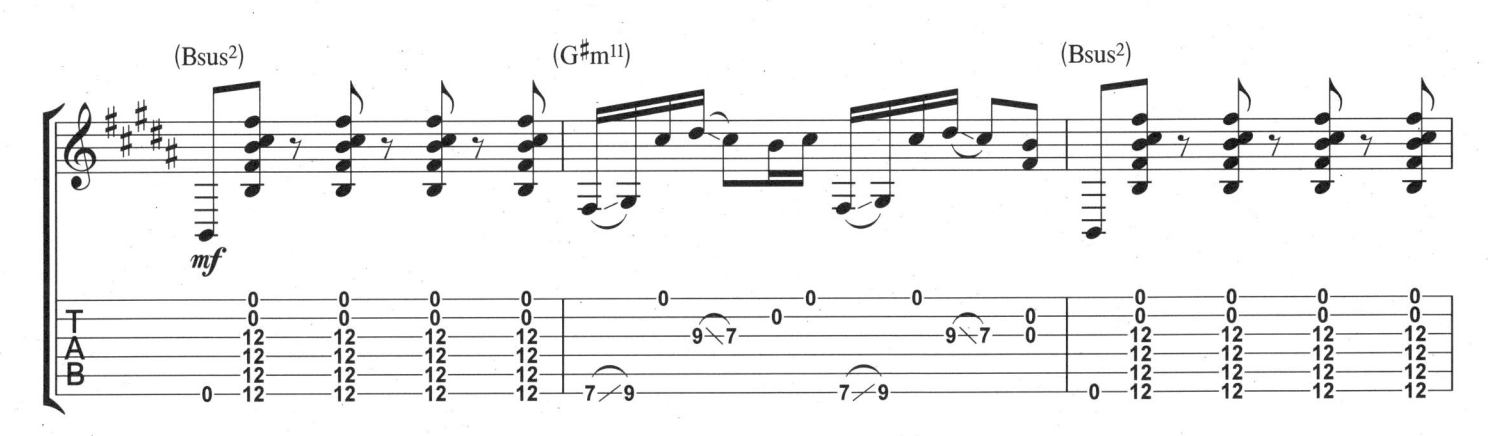

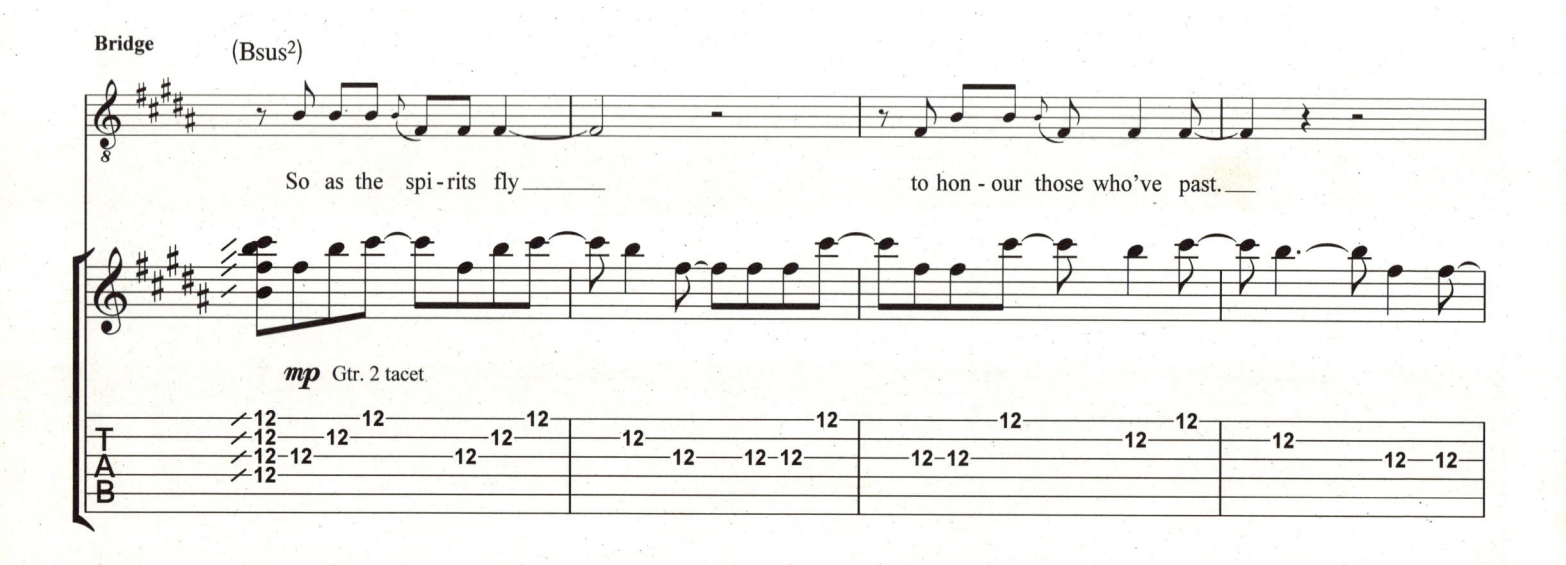

Bridge

So as the spi-rits fly____ to hon-our those who've past.____

We've got to get a-long____ while the time still lasts.____

D.S. al Coda

Coda
(E5)
(F#5)
(G#5)
But I don't un-der-stand how one can kill a man in the name of peace,
(F#5)
(E5)
(F#5)
that's ri-dic-u-lous. But I un-der-stand that I will de-fend
(G#5)
(F#5)
my fa-mi-ly from both sides of mis-er-y.
1.
(D#5)
(E5)
(B5)
Mi-er-ry.
T
A
B

2.
(D#5)
(E5)
(B5)
Mi - er - - - ry.
1.
2.
mp
let ring...
Gtr. 2 plays sim. ad lib.
Outro Solo
mf-f
sim. ad lib. on repeat
TAB

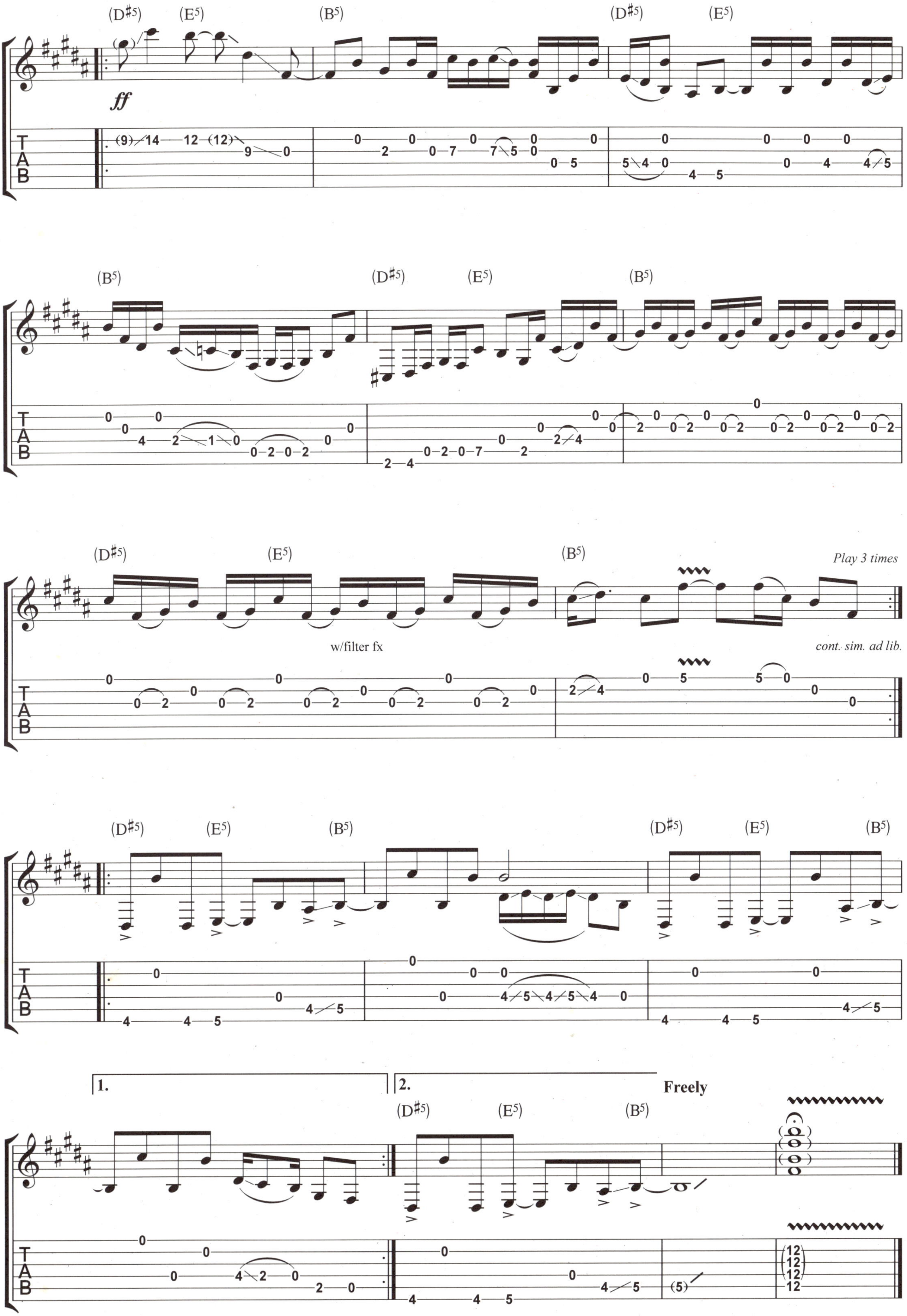
(D♯5)
(E5)
(B5)
ff
Play 3 times
w/filter fx
cont. sim. ad lib.
1.
2.
Freely
TAB

1 2 3 4 5 6 7 8 9

GUITAR TABLATURE EXPLAINED

GUITAR MUSIC CAN BE NOTATED IN THREE DIFFERENT WAYS: ON A MUSICAL STAVE, IN TABLATURE, AND IN RHYTHM SLASHES.

RHYTHM SLASHES: are written above the stave. Strum chords in the rhythm indicated. Round noteheads indicate single notes.

THE MUSICAL STAVE: shows pitches and rhythms and is divided by lines into bars. Pitches are named after the first seven letters of the alphabet.

TABLATURE: graphically represents the guitar fingerboard. Each horizontal line represents a string, and each number represents a fret.

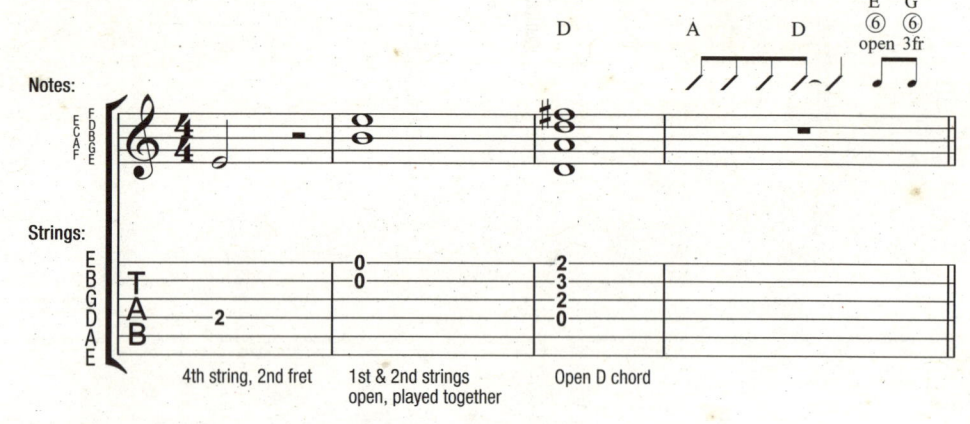

DEFINITIONS FOR SPECIAL GUITAR NOTATION

SEMI-TONE BEND: Strike the note and bend up a semi-tone (½ step).

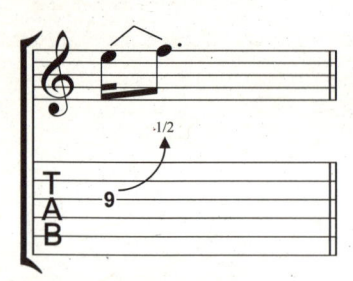

WHOLE-TONE BEND: Strike the note and bend up a whole-tone (full step).

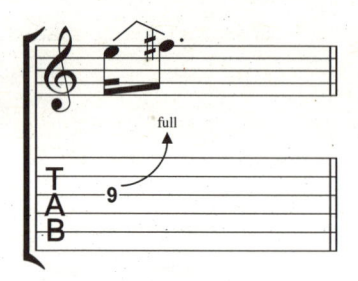

GRACE NOTE BEND: Strike the note and bend as indicated. Play the first note as quickly as possible.

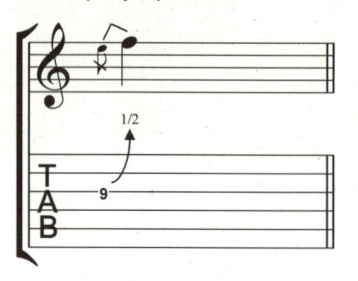

QUARTER-TONE BEND: Strike the note and bend up a ¼ step.

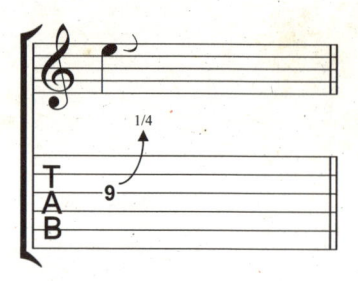

BEND & RELEASE: Strike the note and bend up as indicated, then release back to the original note.

COMPOUND BEND & RELEASE: Strike the note and bend up and down in the rhythm indicated.

PRE-BEND: Bend the note as indicated, then strike it.

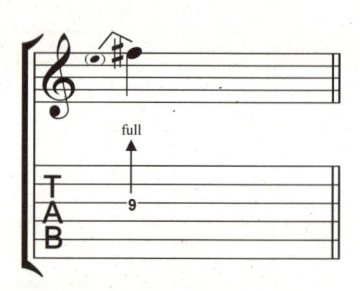

PRE-BEND & RELEASE: Bend the note as indicated. Strike it and release the note back to the original pitch.

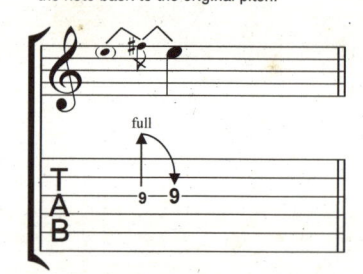

HAMMER-ON: Strike the first note with one finger, then sound the second note (on the same string) with another finger by fretting it without picking.

PULL-OFF: Place both fingers on the note to be sounded, strike the first note and without picking, pull the finger off to sound the second note.

LEGATO SLIDE (GLISS): Strike the first note and then slide the same fret-hand finger up or down to the second note. The second note is not struck.

MUFFLED STRINGS: A percussive sound is produced by laying the first hand across the string(s) without depressing, and striking them with the pick hand.

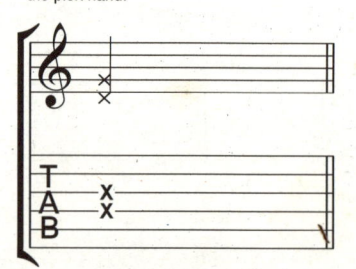

NATURAL HARMONIC: Strike the note while the fret-hand lightly touches the string directly over the fret indicated.

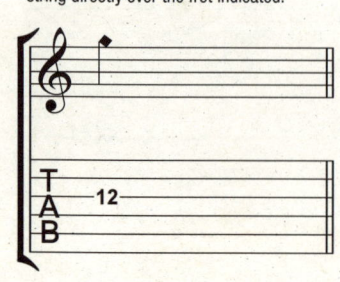

PICK SCRAPE: The edge of the pick is rubbed down (or up) the string, producing a scratchy sound.

PALM MUTING: The note is partially muted by the pick hand lightly touching the string(s) just before the bridge.

SHIFT SLIDE (GLISS & RESTRIKE): Same as legato slide, except the second note is struck.